MODERN
QUILTS
from the BLOGGING
UNIVERSE

MODERN QUILTS
from the BLOGGING UNIVERSE

Martingale®
Create with Confidence

Modern Quilts from the Blogging Universe
© 2012 by Martingale®

Martingale
19021 120th Ave. NE, Ste. 102
Bothell, WA 98011-9511 USA
ShopMartingale.com

Printed in China
17 16 15 14 13 12   8 7 6 5 4 3 2 1

Library of Congress Cataloging-in-Publication Data is available upon request.

ISBN: 978-1-60468-211-3

CREDITS

President & CEO: Tom Wierzbicki
Editor in Chief: Mary V. Green
Design Director: Paula Schlosser
Managing Editor: Karen Costello Soltys
Technical Editor: Nancy Mahoney
Copy Editor: Tiffany Mottet
Production Manager: Regina Girard
Illustrator: Missy Shepler
Cover & Text Designer: Adrienne Smitke
Photographer: Brent Kane

CONTENTS

INTRODUCTION

If you've ever designed, stitched, or admired modern quilts, welcome! You'll feel right at home within these pages. If you've never made a modern quilt before, hold on to your hat—you're in for the quiltmaking adventure of a lifetime.

Modern quilts have spurred a popularity that harkens back to history's other quiltmaking crazes, from early sampler, Amish, and Crazy quilts to more recent obsessions with Civil War, Depression-era, and Gee's Bend designs. It makes perfect sense to include the modern style in quiltmaking's memoirs—after all, modern quiltmakers are the first to acknowledge that many of their works are direct descendants of traditional quilts.

In the context of quilts, "modern" doesn't necessarily mean contemporary. Although the quilts in this book could certainly be categorized as such, this compilation focuses on a specific aesthetic. Designs touch on ideas such as purposeful imperfections; improvisational piecing; exploring negative space; and approaching classic quilt blocks in new ways. That said, one rule of modern quiltmaking reigns: there are no rules.

If there's one thing that sets the modern-quilt movement apart from historical quilting trends, it's the way in which information about it is shared. This specially selected group of designers has spread the word about the modern-quilt movement in the most efficient, most immediate way possible—by blogging about it. This dazzling, diverse collection of quilts comes from some of the blogosphere's best and brightest designers. Along with detailed how-to patterns, these bloggers impart their own stories about their love of modern quiltmaking. They share how they discovered the genre, what their personal designing process is like, and what they think the definition of modern quilt-making is (a hot-button topic!). Whether you feed, follow, email, or tweet, stay in touch with these designers however you can. They're the next generation of quilting leaders. They're the ones to watch.

One thread that connects each designer to the other is the freedom they feel when making modern quilts. Try their patterns; then find your own path to quiltmaking freedom, whether it's inspired by tradition, improvisation, or a combination of the two. Remember—there are no rules!

The modern quiltmaking movement may seem new, but it's already established itself as an important part of quiltmaking history. You, with this book in hand, are a witness to that history. And as you create these designs, you become a participant. Enjoy the journey!

P.S. We wanted to offer you as many step-by-step patterns as we could fit into 96 pages, so we removed our usual section on basic quiltmaking techniques. But no worries—you can find the info on our website, in downloadable form, for free! For detailed instructions about making borders, backings, bindings, and the like, visit ShopMartingale.com/HowtoQuilt.

TREE QUILT

Designed and made by
Jolene Klassen

FINISHED QUILT: 56½" x 77½"
FINISHED BLOCKS: 5" to 8" x 10½"

✱ Happy, scrappy, free-form triangles suggest a forest of trees on a background of various neutral fabrics. This quilt design leaves plenty of room for you to express your own creativity through colors and layout.

MATERIALS

Yardage is based on 42"-wide fabric.

4 yards *total* of assorted light prints for background

37 scraps, at least 4" x 8", of assorted blue, green, and pink prints for trees

⅝ yard of multicolored print for binding

4¾ yards of fabric for backing*

62" x 83" piece of batting

Or see "Optional Pieced Backing" on page 13.

CUTTING

With this type of quilt, I prefer to cut strips or pieces as I need them. However, if you prefer to do all your cutting first, here is an approximate guide, assuming you will be making your quilt with a layout very similar to mine.

From *each* of the assorted scraps, cut:

1 triangle shape, no taller than 8" and no wider than 4" (use a rotary cutter and ruler so the edges are completely straight)

From the assorted light prints, cut *a total of:*

37 rectangles, 11" tall and ranging in width from 5" to 8"

Approximately 20 strips, 1½" to 5" wide x 42"

From the multicolored print, cut:

7 binding strips, 2½" x 42"

BLOCK ASSEMBLY

1. Lay one triangular tree piece on top of one background rectangle. Position the tree how you want it to appear in the completed block.

2. Lay your ruler along the bottom of the tree and cut along the edge of the ruler. Set the bottom background piece aside so you can sew it back on later.

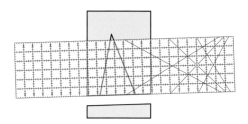

3. Slide the tree approximately ½" to the left of its initial position on the background. Lay your ruler along the right edge of the tree and cut the background fabric along this angle. Set this background piece aside so you can sew it back on later.

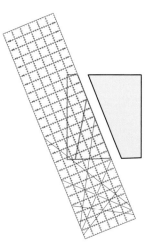

4. Slide your tree to the right so that it extends ½" beyond the edge of the background fabric as shown. Align your ruler along the left edge of the tree and cut the background fabric along this angle. Discard the small triangular background piece underneath the tree.

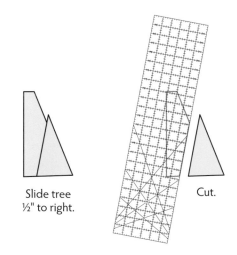

Slide tree ½" to right.

Cut.

5. Lay the tree and the last background piece you cut right sides together along their matching angled edges. Sew them together using a ¼" seam allowance. Press the seam allowances open.

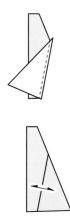

6. Sew the other angled background piece to the tree in the same manner as step 5. Press the seam allowances open.

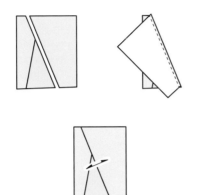

7. Sew the rectangle from step 2 to the bottom edge to complete the block. Press the seam allowances open. Note that the block may not be perfectly rectangular.

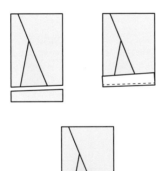

8. Repeat steps 1–7 to make 37 blocks total. Trim your blocks to measure 10½" tall; the width can be any measurement as long as you trim the sides to make them straight and the corners square.

> ## " | Press the Seam Allowances Open or to the Side?
>
> I consider this to be a matter of personal preference and I use a combination of both, depending on what seems to work best in each situation. Pressing the seam allowances open creates a flatter seam and in improvisational designs such as this one, you never know how the blocks will be stitched together. Pressing the seam allowances open also reduces the bulk when you join pieces with multiple angles.

QUILT ASSEMBLY

1. Arrange your tree blocks on a design wall—a piece of batting or flannel pinned to the wall will do. See the "Make It Your Own!" box for ideas when arranging the blocks.

> ## " | Make It Your Own!
>
> Here's where the quilt has a chance to really grow and become your own piece of art. As you make trees, put them on your design wall. Notice what you like or don't like about your trees. Do they have the right amount of contrast to stand out from the background? Do you prefer them tall and skinny or short and squat? Or maybe a combination of both? Do you want a dense forest full of lively trees, or do you prefer a sparsely populated one, as in the quilt I made?
>
> If you're not happy with any of the trees, replace them with ones of different shapes or colors as needed to bring your quilt to life.

2. Once you are pleased with the arrangement of the trees, fill in the spaces between the trees with strips of background fabric.

3. Sew the trees and background pieces together in rows. Press the seam allowances open. Make sure to measure and trim each row to the same length.

> ## " | Keeping the Quilt Square
>
> While working improvisationally is fun, you don't want your quilt tops to be stretched and skewed. By keeping all the rows exactly the same length and pinning before sewing them together, you will ensure that everything remains straight and flat.

4. Join the tree rows, adding scrappy strips of background fabrics between some of the rows as I did. If you do add rows of background strips between the tree rows, be sure to measure and trim these to the same length as the tree rows.

5. For the border, sew background strips together to make two strips approximately 5" x 68" and two strips 5" x 59". Measure the length of the quilt top. Trim the two 68"-long strips to this length and sew them to the sides of the quilt top. Press the seam allowances toward the border. Measure the width of the quilt top and trim the 59"-long strips to this length. Sew these strips to the top and bottom of the quilt top; press. This quilt would look equally nice if you skip the borders and have your trees extending all the way to the edges.

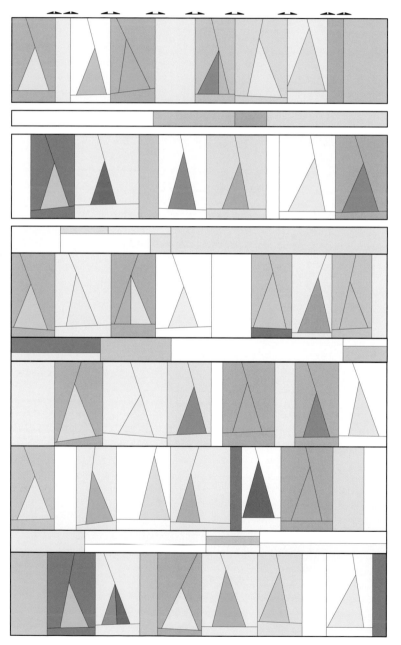

Quilt assembly

FINISHING THE QUILT

For free, downloadable, illustrated how-to instructions on any finishing techniques, go to ShopMartingale.com/HowtoQuilt.

1. Layer the quilt top, batting, and backing; baste the layers together. Quilt as desired.

2. Bind the quilt using the multicolored binding strips. Add a label.

❝ | Optional Pieced Backing

Randomly sew your leftover background pieces together, along with other light fabrics as needed, to make a scrappy back for your quilt.

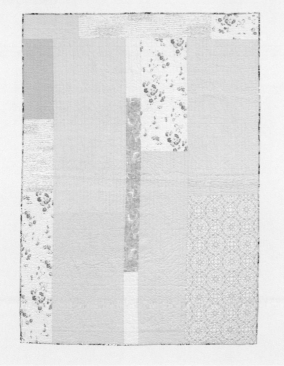

Designer Bio
JOLENE KLASSEN
BlueElephantStitches.blogspot.com

As a child, I watched my mom and grandma sew, and through sewing countless Barbie-doll clothes as well as dresses for myself, I learned to feel at home with needle, thread, and fabric. As a teenager, I worked at a local quilt shop where I learned the basic techniques and was instilled with a love for this medium. As a young mom, I discovered the wealth of inspiration online via quilting blogs.

For a while I was content to soak up, admire, and be inspired by all these quilts made in styles I didn't know even existed. They spoke to me in a way that turned my occasional winter hobby into a full-blown, sneak-into-my-sewing-room-whenever-I-can type of obsession.

Eventually I started my own quilting blog as an extension of my Etsy shop where I sell quilts. It soon became an enjoyable way of interacting with people who shared the love of quilting with me, and I'm very thankful to all of you fellow quilters who have inspired and encouraged me.

While I think that some of my quilts would be labeled as "modern," certainly others would not. I prefer not to set confines on what style of quilts I make. I would rather make what I love. I find myself drawn to designs inspired by traditional or vintage quilt blocks, but interpreted in fresh ways.

JUICY

Designed and made by
Monica Solorio-Snow

FINISHED QUILT: 60½" x 84½"
FINISHED BLOCKS: 6" x 6"

✳ I wanted to design a quilt that would be fun to make while sewing with friends—something enjoyable and simple without too many instructions, allowing me to participate in all the juicy chatter with my pals and still be able to sew without having to focus too much.

MATERIALS

Yardage is based on 42"-wide fabric. Fat quarters measure 18" x 21".

10 fat quarters of assorted prints for blocks

2⅜ yards of gray solid for flying-geese border, Hourglass blocks, and binding

2¼ yards of white solid for background and Hourglass blocks

5¼ yards of fabric for backing

66" x 90" piece of batting

CUTTING

From *each* of 9 assorted fat quarters, cut:
6 squares, 6½" x 6½" (54 total)

From the 1 remaining fat quarter, cut:
5 squares, 6½" x 6½"

From the white solid, cut:
6 strips, 7¼" x 42"; cut into 29 squares, 7¼" x 7¼". Cut each square into quarters diagonally to yield 116 triangles.
9 strips, 3½" x 42"; cut into:
    20 rectangles, 3½" x 6½"
    52 squares, 3½" x 3½"

From the gray solid, cut:
6 strips, 7¼" x 42"; cut into 29 squares, 7¼" x 7¼". Cut each square into quarters diagonally to yield 116 triangles.
4 strips, 3½" x 42"; cut into 24 rectangles, 3½" x 6½"
8 binding strips, 2½" x 42"

BLOCK ASSEMBLY

The fun part about this quilt is that it looks complicated, but it's constructed of two basic units: squares and rectangles.

Flying-Geese Units

1. Place a white square on one corner of a gray rectangle, right sides together. Stitch a diagonal line from corner to corner as shown. Trim the excess corner fabric, leaving a ¼" seam allowance. Press the seam allowances toward the resulting white triangle.

2. Repeat step 1, sewing a white square on the other end of the gray rectangle. Trim and press to complete a flying-geese unit. Make 24 units.

Make 24.

Hourglass Blocks

1. With right sides together, sew a gray triangle and a white triangle together along their short edges as shown. Press the seam allowances toward the gray triangle. Make 116.

Make 116.

2. Join two units to make an Hourglass block, using the opposing seams to nest the units into place for a nice, snug fit. Press the seam allowances to one side. Make 58 blocks.

Make 58.

QUILT ASSEMBLY

1. Referring to the assembly diagram, sew two white squares, five flying-geese units, and four white rectangles together to make the top row. Press the seam allowances toward the white squares and rectangles. Repeat to make the bottom row.

2. Join two flying-geese units, five assorted print squares, and four Hourglass blocks to make a row. Press the seam allowances toward the assorted squares. Make seven rows.

3. Join two white rectangles, five Hourglass blocks, and four assorted print squares to make a row. Press the seam allowances toward the white rectangles and assorted squares. Make six of these rows.

4. Join the rows to complete the quilt top. Press the seam allowances in one direction.

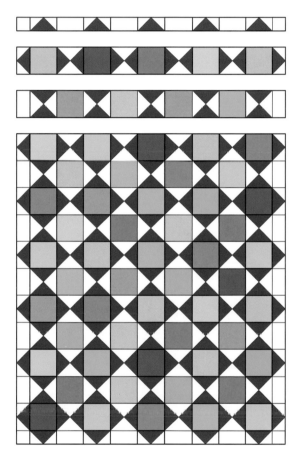

Quilt assembly

FINISHING THE QUILT

For free, downloadable, illustrated how-to instructions on any finishing techniques, go to ShopMartingale.com/HowtoQuilt.

1. Layer the quilt top, batting, and backing; baste the layers together. Quilt as desired.

2. Bind the quilt using the gray binding strips. Add a label.

Unsupervised and armed with sewing needles

Designer Bio
MONICA SOLORIO-SNOW
TheHappyZombie.com/blog

I'm a lover of quilts, fabric, stitchery, and zombies. I keep busy as a fabric designer, quilt pattern writer, and graphic designer. My addictions and my fuel are my family and friends; quilting, sewing, and crafting; Pinterest and Flickr; anything buttered; coffee and ice-cold milk.

I'm a first generation American, and there's no quilting history in my background—no quilts from my grandmothers, no treasures in the attic to be found. So the art and tradition of quilting starts with me, and quilting is what makes me feel connected to America's past.

As in the 1930s, we've been facing some tough economic times—so we're using what we have, and stretching what we have (or bought) to make it go further. I get so excited when I see an antique quilt that's been frugally backed with chicken-feed bagging—the printed brand name still visible. There's real beauty in frugality.

Another correlation between 1930s quilts and modern quilts is that they're not just beautiful works of art, but serve as vehicles for snuggling and cuddling, warmth and comfort—quilts that are meant to be used. *Utilitarian* is not a very pretty or glamorous word, but if you squint your eyes . . . it looks like Utopia. In my Utopia, the quilts run amok and spread love and happiness.

STARFLOWER

Designed and made by
Angela Nash

FINISHED QUILT: 60" x 60"
FINISHED BLOCKS: 8½" x 8½"

✳ Modern quilters often talk about negative space. I thought it would be interesting to play around with reversing that negative space by starting with a modern block. I enjoy piecing and swapping the placement of prints and the neutral background. The end result is fun and sometimes surprising. Here the white, wonky stars fade into the background and the fun print flowers emerge.

I sized this quilt to take the best advantage of a collection of fat quarters.

MATERIALS

Yardage is based on 42"-wide fabric. Fat quarters measure 18" x 21".

3½ yards of white solid for blocks
5 fat quarters of assorted pink prints for blocks
3 fat quarters of assorted yellow prints for blocks
3 fat quarters of assorted orange prints for blocks
⅝ yard of deep-pink solid for binding
3¾ yards of fabric for backing*
66" x 66" piece of batting

*Or see "Optional Pieced Backing" on page 21.

CUTTING

From the white solid, cut:
9 squares, 9" x 9"
40 squares, 9" x 9"; cut each square in half diagonally
    to yield 80 triangles

From *each* fat quarter, cut:
4 squares, 9" x 9" (44 total)

From the deep-pink solid, cut:
7 binding strips, 2½" x 42"

💬 | Fixing a Short Fat Quarter

If you have a fat quarter that isn't quite 18" wide, some of your squares will be a tad smaller than 9". You can make up for it with the white triangles by positioning the triangles so that their bottoms extend past the edge of the square. Then the completed block can be squared up to the correct size.

BLOCK ASSEMBLY

1. From your prints, choose 10 yellow squares, 18 pink squares, and 12 orange squares. The extra two yellow and two pink squares will not be needed; set these aside for another project or to use on the quilt back.

2. Place a white triangle on one corner of a yellow, pink, or orange square at any angle you like. Make sure the triangle hangs over the edge at least ½" so that the corner is fully covered.

3. Flip the white triangle along the diagonal edge as shown and stitch using a ¼" seam allowance.

4. Open the triangle and make sure the corner of the square is fully covered. Fold the triangle back and trim the excess corner fabric, cutting along the edge of the white triangle.

5. Press the seam allowances open. Do not trim the extra white fabric yet. Make 40 units. Vary the size and angle of the white triangles for fun, wonky interest.

Make 40.

❝ | Chain Piecing

Once you have a feel for what angles appeal to you in the star points, you can position the white triangles on the assorted squares and chain piece them, sewing all the units first. Then trim and press all 40 units.

6. Repeat steps 2–5, stitching a white triangle to an adjacent corner of each unit from step 5. Make 40 blocks and trim each block to measure 9" x 9".

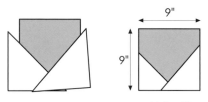

Make 40.

QUILT ASSEMBLY

1. Lay out the nine white squares and the star-point blocks as shown in the assembly diagram, paying attention to the orientation of the star points on each block.

2. Being careful to keep the blocks in order and oriented correctly, sew them together in rows. Press the seam allowances open. Join the rows; press.

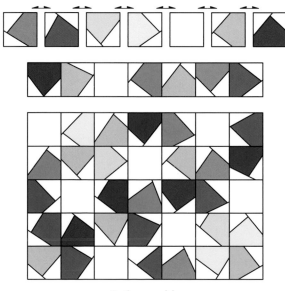

Quilt assembly

FINISHING THE QUILT

For free, downloadable, illustrated how-to instructions on any finishing techniques, go to ShopMartingale.com/HowtoQuilt.

1. Layer the quilt top, batting, and backing; baste the layers together. Quilt as desired.

2. Bind the quilt using the deep-pink binding strips. Add a label.

" | Optional Pieced Backing

1. From each leftover fat quarter, cut one 3" x 18" rectangle. Cut the leftover 9" squares into 3" x 9" rectangles. (If your strips are narrower than 3", just make sure they are all the *same* width and cut the 42"-long pieces wider in step 2.) Join the rectangles, end to end, to make three strips at least 66" long. Then join the three strips along their long edges to make an 8"-wide pieced strip.

2. From a solid, cut one 40" x 66" piece and two 20" x 42" pieces for backing. Trim the selvage off one end of each 20"-wide backing piece, then sew the pieces end to end. Press the seam allowances open and trim to 20" x 66".

3. Join the solid backing pieces and the pieced strip to complete the quilt back.

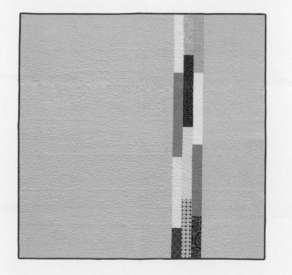

My Three Sons

...and the crafting I get done in between all the activity of three very busy boys.

Designer Bio
ANGELA NASH
MyThreeSonsKnit.blogspot.com

I've always made things—clothes for my dolls, Halloween costumes, and more. Through crafting and knitting, I found the blog world and happened upon some cute I-spy quilts. My boys were little and I thought an I-spy quilt would be a fun project to try. I had no intention of making any other quilts. As I went searching for fun fabrics, I discovered so many fun, modern prints that I suddenly found myself buying more fabrics and following modern-quilt blogs.

As a mechanical engineer, my approach to quilt design involves lots of math. I enjoy using a calculator, ruler, and colored pencils to sketch out shapes. I'm also constantly searching for new things to learn—from techniques to color theory to exploring combinations of blocks and fabrics.

Having my own blog has been an essential part of my growth in both skill and style. It's a wonderful log of my journey and encouraging to look back and see what I've accomplished when I'm stuck in the weeds of a difficult skill or design that just won't come together. More important are the modern-quilt friends whom I've met through my blog. Helping push me to the next level, they celebrate the process, offer suggestions and tips on color or construction, and join me in the joy of a finished project, fully understanding the whole creative journey.

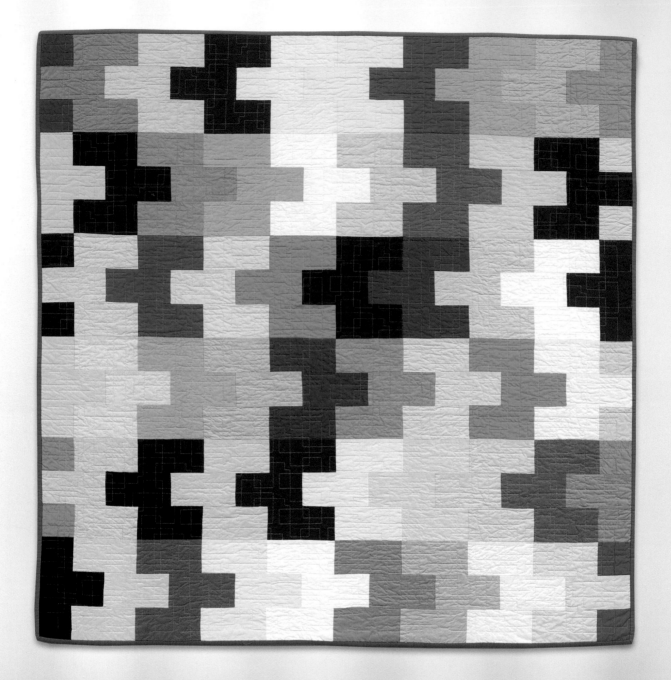

JIGSAW

Designed and pieced by Amy Ellis;
quilted by Natalia Bonner

FINISHED QUILT: 54½" x 54½"

✳ This project makes a great use of fat quarters or scraps! Simply cut your pieces and assemble the columns for a quick quilt, one that's sure to be loved.

MATERIALS

Yardage is based on 42"-wide fabric. Fat quarters measure 18" x 21".

¼ yard or 1 fat quarter *each* of 20 assorted solids*
½ yard of blue solid for binding
3½ yards of fabric for backing
60" x 60" piece of batting

Amy used Robert Kaufman Kona Cotton in the following colors: Snow, Bubble Gum, Midnight, Ruby, Cheddar, Amber, Lemon, Corn Yellow, Green Tea, Grass Green, Ice Frappe, Lagoon, Bluebell, Regatta, Lilac, Bright Peri, Ash, Tan, Earth, and Espresso.

CUTTING

From *each* of 12 solids, cut:
2 strips, 3½" x 42"; cut into:
    7 rectangles, 3½" x 6½" (84 total)
    2 squares, 3½" x 3½" (24 total)

From *each* of the remaining 8 solids, cut:
2 strips, 3½" x 42"; cut into 9 rectangles, 3½" x 6½" (72 total)

From the blue solid, cut:
6 binding strips, 2½" x 42"

> ❝ | **Don't Be Mixed Up!**
>
> When cutting solids, I like to open my strips before crosscutting the squares and rectangles. This way I always know which side is up. To lay out this quilt, group like-colored pieces in threes and pin them together as a unit. The squares will pair with one rectangle. This will help you decide on color placement and assemble the quilt efficiently.

QUILT ASSEMBLY

This quilt is assembled in rows, and there are no blocks to piece.

1. To find a pleasing arrangement of color, lay out the solid rectangles and squares in six rows on a design wall. Each row will have three strips and consist of 10 colors, with a square/rectangle group at both ends of each row. Once you have found a nice arrangement, stack the rows and move to the sewing machine.

2. To keep your colors in order, and avoid confusion, chain piece across each strip. Press the seam allowances as shown. At the end of rows 1, 3, and 5, one rectangle will not be used. Likewise, at the beginning of rows 2, 4, and 6, one rectangle will not be used.

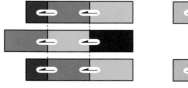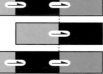

Rows 1, 3, and 5   Rows 2, 4, and 6

3. After pressing, clip the threads between two chain-pieced strips in a row, then line up the top and bottom edges to stagger the pieces. Use a few pins, to ensure even distribution, and sew the two strips together. In the same way, sew the strip to the other side of the row and press the seam allowances to one side. Repeat to make six rows total.

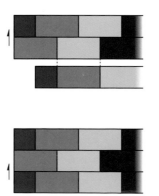

Make 6 rows.

4. Nesting the seams, join the rows to complete the quilt top. Press seam allowances in one direction.

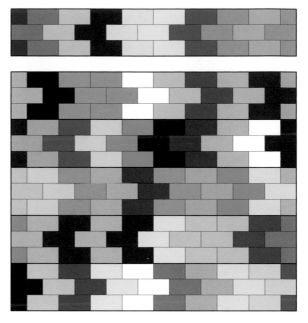

Quilt assembly

FINISHING THE QUILT

For free, downloadable, illustrated how-to instructions on any finishing techniques, go to ShopMartingale.com/HowtoQuilt.

1. Layer the quilt top, batting, and backing; baste the layers together. Quilt as desired.

2. Bind the quilt using the blue binding strips. Add a label.

" | Make It a Twin

MATERIALS

To make a twin-size quilt, measuring 72" x 96", you will need:

½ yard *each* of 20 assorted solids

¾ yard of blue solid for binding

6½ yards of fabric for backing

78" x 102" piece of batting

CUTTING

Refer to "Don't Be Mixed Up!" on page 23.

From *each* of 16 fabrics, cut:

4 strips, 3½" x 42"; cut into:
    19 rectangles, 3½" x 6½" (304 total; 8 are extra)
    2 squares, 3½" x 3½" (36 total)

From *each* of 4 fabrics, cut:

3 strips, 3½" x 42"; cut into 18 rectangles, 3½" x 6½" (72 total)

From the blue solid, cut:

9 binding strips, 2½" x 42"

QUILT ASSEMBLY

On a design wall or other flat surface, lay out the solid rectangles and squares in eight rows as shown in the assembly diagram below. Each row will have three strips and consist of 17 colors, with a square/rectangle group at both ends of each row. Once you have a pleasing arrangement, assemble the quilt as described on page 24.

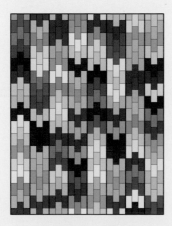

Quilt assembly

Designer Bio
AMY ELLIS
AmysCreativeSide.com

When I first discovered the blog community, I was amazed at finding a great source of inspiration and abundance of knowledge. I wanted to be a part of it and began blogging in March 2008. *Amy's Creative Side* has become my outlet, and a point of connection with thousands of readers (and friends) on a daily basis. I share current projects, including quilts, bags, the occasional garment, reviews of products used, and little bits of family life. As a wife and mom, my husband and four kids are never far from my thoughts as I write.

Through blogging, I have encountered many opportunities. I'm proud to have authored two books with Martingale, and contributed to three others. I'm constantly looking around me for my next quilt design, knowing that inspiration can strike at any moment.

I love encouraging the online community as well. Each week I feature a different blogger who has participated in my biannual online festival, and encourage my readers to get to know someone new. The Bloggers' Quilt Festival started as a simple idea, and each time I host the festival I am inspired by the variety of quilts, and the stories that are shared along with each one. There's no judging or required skill set for entry, so it's more like a big party online. Look for the Bloggers' Quilt Festival at: http://amyscreativeside.com/bloggers-quilt-festival.

INDIAN SUMMER

Designed and pieced by Katy Jones;
quilted by Tia Curtis

FINISHED QUILT: 48½" x 48½"
FINISHED BLOCKS: 17" x 17"

✳ I'm always drawn to traditional quilt blocks and patterns, and my absolute favorite of all is the Dresden plate. It's such a fantastically versatile block, and when combined with hand appliqué it makes a wonderful on-the-go project. What makes it even better is that it's much simpler than it looks, but has a truly heirloom quality about it. The rich color scheme reminds me of a late summer day, when everything in the garden is at its fullest and brightest and balmy evenings can be spent sitting in the twilight, stitching.

MATERIALS

Yardage is based on 42"-wide fabric.

1⅝ yards of gray solid for background, Dresden plate centers, and binding

1⅝ yards of large-scale floral for outer border*

1¼ yards *total* of assorted scraps for Dresden plate blades and circle appliqués (try to use at least 16 different prints; scraps should be at least 3" x 6")

½ yard of pink solid for blocks

½ yard of blue print for sashing and inner border

3⅛ yards of fabric for backing

54" x 54" piece of batting

9" x 12" piece of fusible web

Freezer paper

*Yardage amount is for one-piece lengthwise-cut border strips. If you don't mind seams in your outer border, ¾ yard is sufficient to cut crosswise strips.

CUTTING

Patterns for the wedge and circle templates are on pages 30–31.

From the assorted scraps, cut *a total of*:
80 wedges
1 square, 2½" x 2½"
Set aside the remaining scraps for small circles.

From the gray solid, cut:
2 strips, 15½" x 42"; cut into 4 squares, 15½" x 15½"
6 binding strips, 2½" x 42"
Set aside the remaining fabric for large circles.

From the pink solid, cut:
8 strips, 1½" x 15½"
8 strips, 1½" x 17½"

From the blue print, cut:
4 strips, 2½" x 17½"
2 strips, 2½" x 34½"
2 strips, 2½" x 40½"

From the *lengthwise grain* of the large-scale floral, cut:
2 strips, 4½" x 43"
2 strips, 4½" x 51" (or 5 strips, 4½" x 42", from the crosswise grain)

BLOCK ASSEMBLY

1. Fold each wedge shape in half, right sides together, and sew across the wider end using a ¼" seam allowance. You can chain piece these seams to speed up the process and save thread.

2. Turn the wedge right side out and use a bluntly pointed object (like a knitting needle or chopstick) to push the tip out so it's pointy and the piece is blade shaped. Press the blade flat. Make 80.

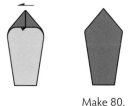

Make 80.

3. Lay out four circles of 20 blades each, taking care to not have similar fabrics close to each other. Rearrange until you have a good flow of value or colors. Aligning the shoulders of the blades, sew the blades together using a ¼" seam allowance to make a ring. (The bottoms will be covered by the circle appliqué, so if they don't match up exactly, no one will know.) Press all seam allowances in one direction. Make four.

Align.

Make 4.

4. Fold a gray square in half vertically and horizontally, and press lightly with an iron to establish centering lines. Unfold and use the pressed lines to center a ring of blades. Pin the ring to the gray square and sew in place, using either a machine blanket or zigzag stitch or by hand sewing using a slip stitch. Make four blocks.

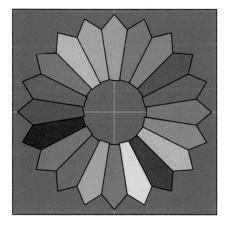

Make 4.

5. Trace the large-circle template onto freezer paper or cardstock and cut out four circles. Lightly press the freezer-paper circles to the wrong side of the gray solid. Cut out four gray circles, adding approximately ¼" allowance all around each one as shown.

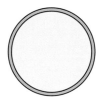

6. Using your fingers, firmly press the seam allowance over the freezer-paper template. Lightly press with an iron if needed. Fold the circle into quarters and press lightly with an iron. Repeat the process with each circle.

Make 4.

7. Unfold and center the circle on top of a ring, using the pressed lines as a guide. Pin and stitch as before. Repeat for all four blocks.

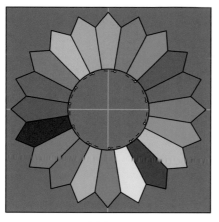

Make 4.

8. On the wrong side of each block, use small, sharp scissors to carefully cut a snip in the gray fabric behind the appliquéd circle. *Do not* cut into the freezer-paper template. Then carefully cut away the excess fabric, leaving at least a ¼" seam allowance. Make sure you do not cut into the stitches or through the appliquéd circle. Peel away and discard the paper template. Gently press each block.

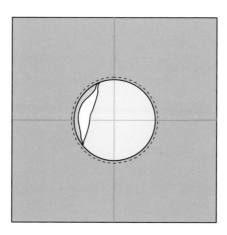

9. Sew 1½" x 15½" pink-solid strips to the top and bottom of each block. Press the seam allowances toward the pink strips. Sew 1½" x 17½" pink-solid strips to the remaining sides of each block. Press the seam allowances toward the pink strips. Make four blocks each measuring 17½" x 17½".

10. Using the small-circle template, trace 24 circles onto the paper side of the fusible web. Roughly cut out these circles, leaving about a ¼" margin all around the marked line. Following the manufacturer's instructions, fuse a circle, fusible-web side down, on the wrong side of each appliqué fabric. Cut out the fabric circles on the drawn line.

11. On two of the blocks, fuse 12 small circles on each block, arranging them in sets of three as shown. Machine stitch around each circle; I used a straight stitch so that the edges would become frayed with use and washing, for a vintage look. You could use a zigzag or blanket stitch, or even hand stitch with embroidery thread.

QUILT ASSEMBLY

1. Referring to the assembly diagram on page 30, sew two blocks and one blue 2½" x 17½" strip together to make a block row. Press the seam allowances toward the blue strip. Make a second block row.

2. Sew the two remaining blue 2½" x 17½" strips and the 2½" square together to make a sashing row. Press the seam allowances toward the blue strips.

3. Join the block rows and sashing row to complete the quilt center. Press the seam allowances toward the sashing row.

4. For the inner border, sew the blue 2½" x 34½" strips to the sides of the quilt top. Press the seam allowances toward the border. Sew the blue 2½" x 40½" strips to the top and bottom of the quilt top; press.

5. For the outer border, measure the length of the quilt top. Trim the two floral 43"-long strips to this length and sew them to the sides of the quilt top. Press the seam allowances toward the border. Measure the width of the quilt top and trim the floral 51"-long strips to this measurement. Sew these strips to the top and bottom of the quilt top; press.

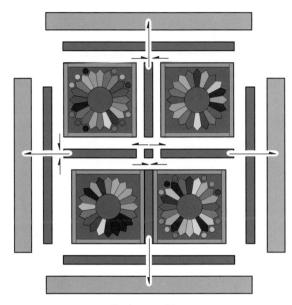

Quilt assembly

" | Adding Borders

Mark the centers of the border strips and the centers of the sides of the quilt top. Matching centers and ends, pin the borders to the sides of the quilt top. As you pin, prevent the strips from stretching by pinning from the center to each end.

FINISHING THE QUILT

For free, downloadable, illustrated how-to instructions on any finishing techniques, go to ShopMartingale.com/HowtoQuilt.

1. Layer the quilt top, batting, and backing; baste the layers together. Quilt as desired.

2. Bind the quilt using the gray binding strips. Add a label.

Large circle
Make 4.

Flip pattern along this line to make a complete circle.

Wedge
Make 80.

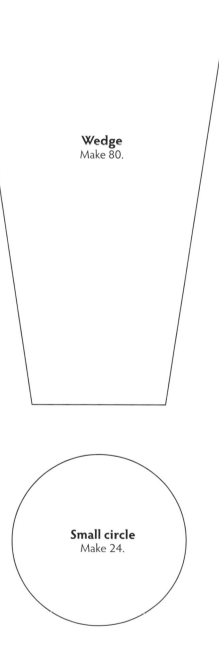

Small circle
Make 24.

Designer Bio
KATY JONES
ImAGingerMonkey.blogspot.com

I'm British and live in a little hamlet in West
Yorkshire with my husband, two children,
two cats, and a dog. I was first introduced to
quilting in early 2008 after forming a trans-
atlantic friendship on Flickr, although I had
spent most of life being a little crafty in one
way or another. My passion for the history,
traditions, and art of quilting developed my
signature style, which is neither modern nor
traditional, but rather a little of both.

In 2010, I cofounded the popular modern
quilting eMagazine *Fat Quarterly* with a group
of like-minded quilters who were keen to
build on the values of an old-fashioned quilting community via the modern medium of the
Internet. The magazine continues to grow,
and with it the community that it holds as its
core element.

I feel you should be true to yourself. Let
your own personality shine through in both
your blog and your work. You are one of a
kind, so don't follow the rest of the fold. Be
you and your work will be better as a result.

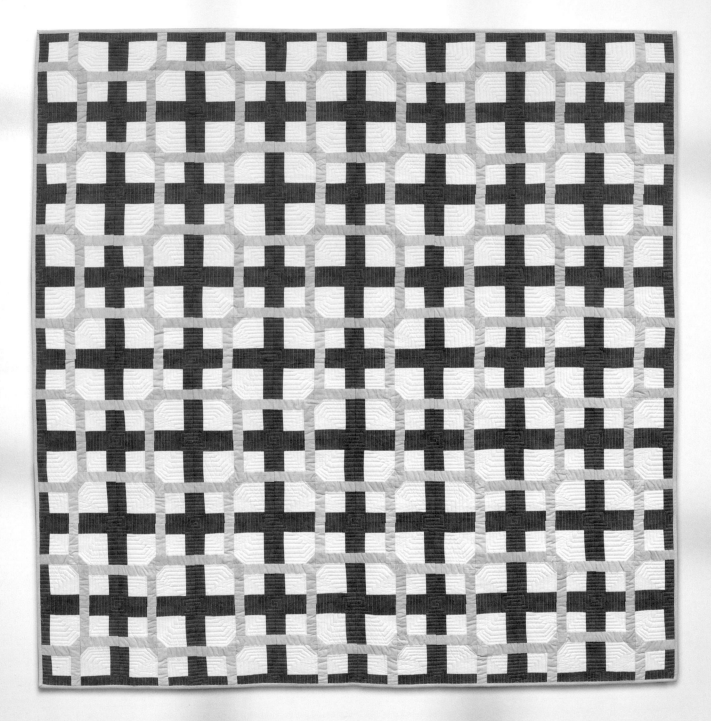

KNOTS

Designed and machine quilted
by Natalia Bonner;
pieced by Ilene Peterson;
bound by Kathleen Whiting

FINISHED QUILT: 60½" x 60½"
FINISHED BLOCKS: 7½" x 7½"

⭐ This quilt is a fun and simple design made from just one block. While this version of "Knots" is made from all solids, it would be very cute when made from prints as well.

MATERIALS

Yardage is based on 42"-wide fabric.

2 yards of gray solid for blocks
1¾ yards of ivory solid for blocks
1⅜ yards of blue solid for blocks and binding
1 yard of yellow solid for blocks
3¾ yards of fabric for backing
66" x 66" piece of batting

CUTTING

From the yellow solid, cut:
3 strips, 3¼" x 42"; cut into 64 rectangles, 1½" x 3¼"
3 strips, 4¼" x 42"; cut into 64 rectangles, 1½" x 4¼"
3 strips, 1½" x 42"; cut into 64 squares, 1½" x 1½"

From the ivory solid, cut:
11 strips, 3¼" x 42"; cut into 128 squares, 3¼" x 3¼"
8 strips, 2¼" x 42"; cut into 128 squares, 2¼" x 2¼"

From the gray solid, cut:
10 strips, 3¼" x 42"; cut into 256 rectangles, 1½" x 3¼"
5 strips, 4¼" x 42"; cut into 128 rectangles, 1½" x 4¼"
5 strips, 2¼" x 42"; cut into 128 rectangles, 1½" x 2¼"

From the blue solid, cut:
3 strips, 3¼" x 42"; cut into 64 rectangles, 1½" x 3¼"
3 strips, 4¼" x 42"; cut into 64 rectangles, 1½" x 4¼"
3 strips, 1½" x 42"; cut into 64 squares, 1½" x 1½"
7 binding strips, 2½" x 42"

BLOCK ASSEMBLY

1. Place a yellow 1½" square on one corner of an ivory 3¼" square, right sides together. Stitch a diagonal line as shown. Trim the excess corner fabric, leaving a ¼" seam allowance. Press the seam allowances toward the resulting yellow triangle. Make 64 yellow units. In the same way, sew a blue 1½" square on one corner of each remaining ivory 3¼" square to make 64 blue units.

Make 64 of each.

2. Sew a gray 1½" x 3¼" rectangle to the left edge of each yellow unit and each blue unit from step 1. Press the seam allowances toward the gray rectangle. Make 64 of each unit.

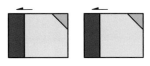

Make 64 of each.

3. Sew a gray 1½" x 4¼" rectangle to the bottom of each yellow unit and each blue unit. Press the seam allowances toward the gray rectangle. Make 64 of each unit.

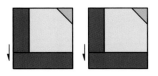

Make 64 of each.

4. Sew a gray 1½" x 2¼" rectangle to the right edge of an ivory 2¼" square. Press the seam allowances toward the gray rectangle. Make 128.

Make 128.

5. Sew a gray 1½" x 3¼" rectangle to the bottom of each unit from step 4. Press the seam allowances toward the newly added rectangle. Make 128.

Make 128.

6. Add a blue 1½" x 3¼" rectangle to the top of 64 of the units from step 5. Sew a yellow 1½" x 3¼" rectangle to the top of the remaining 64 units. Press the seam allowances toward the newly added rectangle.

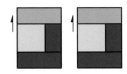

Make 64 of each.

7. Sew a yellow 1½" x 4¼" rectangle to the left side of each blue unit from step 6. Sew a blue 1½" x 4¼" rectangle to the left side of each yellow unit. Press the seam allowances toward the newly added rectangle. Keep like units in separate piles.

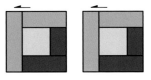

Make 64 of each.

8. Sew the units from step 7 to the units from step 3 to make half blocks as shown. Make 64 of each. Press the seam allowances toward the blue or yellow rectangle. Again, keep like units together.

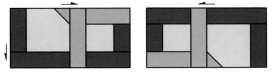

Make 64 of each.

9. Using a half block from each pile, join the half blocks to complete the block as shown. Press the seam allowances to one side. Make 64 blocks.

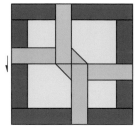

Make 64.

QUILT ASSEMBLY

1. Arrange the blocks according to the assembly diagram, rotating them as shown to create the secondary design. Sew the blocks together in rows. Press the seam allowances in opposite directions from row to row.

2. Join the rows. Press the seam allowances in one direction.

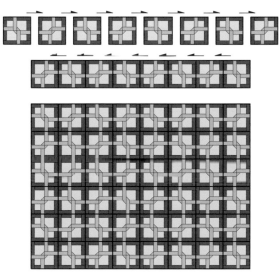

Quilt assembly

FINISHING THE QUILT

For free, downloadable, illustrated how-to instructions on any finishing techniques, go to ShopMartingale.com/HowtoQuilt.

1. Layer the quilt top, batting, and backing; baste the layers together. Quilt as desired.

2. Bind the quilt using the blue binding strips. Add a label.

Designer Bio
NATALIA BONNER
PieceandQuilt.com

I've been piecing as long as I can remember. As a young girl, I watched my mom piece quilts, home decor, and clothing and was so fascinated by it. In 2007, while pregnant, I got a crazy idea to quit my job and take on the quilting world full time. I didn't even own a conventional machine, but I purchased a Gammill long-arm quilting machine and have never looked back.

I now spend my time machine quilting for others and myself, designing quilts, taking care of my children, and blogging about my journey. I began blogging shortly after purchasing my long-arm machine, mostly to share my quilting with family who lived out of state. I had no idea there was such an amazing blogging community, so many friends to make, and so much knowledge to gain from other bloggers.

I love to share my quilts, projects that I've machine quilted for my customers, and many other ideas through tutorials. My work has been published in *American Patchwork and Quilting* magazine, *Quiltmaker* magazine, and *Modern Basics* by Amy Ellis (Martingale, 2010). Visit my blog to check out many of my free tutorials and to learn more about my published work, including my book on free-motion quilting.

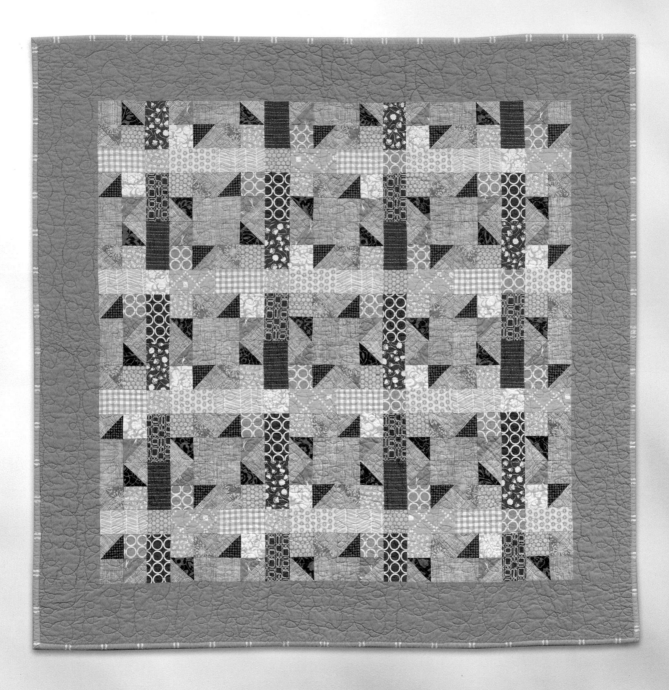

MINI CLAW THROW

Designed and made by
Jeni Baker

FINISHED QUILT: 51½" x 51½"
FINISHED BLOCKS: 10" x 10"

✂ Here's a modern twist on the traditional Bear Claw block—when you set the blocks together without sashing, these fun blocks create stars right before your eyes.

MATERIALS

Yardage is based on 42"-wide fabric.

¼ yard *each* of 4 assorted yellow prints for blocks and sashing squares
¼ yard *each* of 4 assorted teal prints for blocks
¼ yard *each* of 4 assorted aqua prints for sashing
¼ yard *each* of 4 assorted dark-gray prints for sashing
1 yard of gray solid for border
⅞ yard of light-gray print for background
½ yard of yellow print for binding
3¼ yards of fabric for backing*
57" x 57" piece of batting

Or see "Optional Pieced Backing" on page 40.

CUTTING

From the light-gray print, cut:
64 squares, 2½" x 2½"
64 squares, 3" x 3"

From *each* of the teal prints, cut:
16 squares, 3" x 3" (64 total)

From *each* of the yellow prints, cut:
20 squares, 2½" x 2½" (80 total)

From *each* of the aqua prints, cut:
8 rectangles, 2½" x 4½" (32 total)

From *each* of the dark-gray prints, cut:
8 rectangles, 2½" x 4½" (32 total)

From the gray solid, cut:
5 strips, 6" x 42"

From the yellow print, cut:
6 binding strips, 2½" x 42"

BLOCK ASSEMBLY

1. Mark a diagonal line on the wrong side of each light-gray 3" square. Layer the marked square with a teal square, right sides together, and stitch ¼" on each side of the marked line. Cut the squares apart on the line to make two half-square-triangle units. Press the seam allowances toward the teal triangle. Trim the units to measure 2½" x 2½". Make 128 units total.

Make 128.

2. Lay out two half-square-triangle units, one yellow square, and one light-gray 2½" square as shown. Sew the pieces into rows. Press the seam allowances toward the squares. Join the rows and press. Make 64.

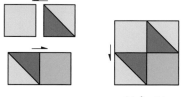

Make 64.

3. Sew two units from step 2 to opposite sides of an aqua rectangle as shown. Press the seam allowances open. Make 32.

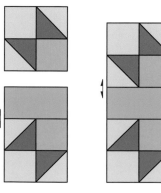

Make 32.

4. Join two dark-gray rectangles and one yellow square as shown. Press the seam allowances open. Make 16.

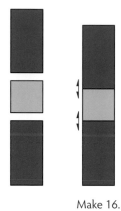

Make 16.

5. Join two units from step 3 and one unit from step 4 as shown to make a block. Press the seam allowances open. Make 16 blocks.

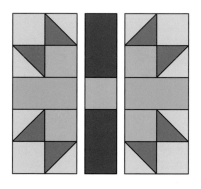

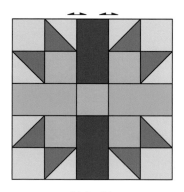

Make 16.

" | **Assembly-Line Sewing**

If you sew the blocks in assembly-line style, rather than making one block at a time, you'll find the blocks go together a little bit faster.

QUILT ASSEMBLY

1. Arrange the blocks in four rows of four blocks each. Sew the blocks together in rows. Press the seam allowances in opposite directions from row to row. Join the rows. Press the seam allowances in one direction.

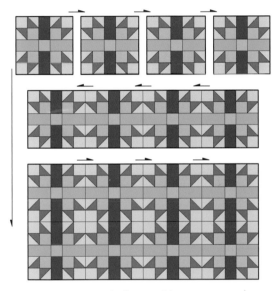

Quilt assembly

Designer Bio
JENI BAKER
InColorOrder.blogspot.com

I love nothing more than to be surrounded by fabric. I taught myself to sew with a little help from my mother, and for years I only sewed tote bags. When I went away to school, I made my first quilt and have been hooked ever since. In addition to sewing, my hobbies include photography, baking, and collecting vintage kitchenware and linens. I currently live in Wisconsin with my pet bunny, George.

My favorite part of the sewing process is fabric and color selection. I love reinventing traditional patterns in fresh modern colors, and I'm constantly inspired by the vintage quilts I discover in my local antique shops as well as online. I think most modern quilt patterns can be traced back to traditional or vintage quilts in some way. The construction techniques may be different, but most of the designs have been around for a long time.

You can find me blogging about my sewing adventures and color process. Because of my blog, I was able to teach "Fabric and Color Selection" at the first annual Sewing Summit conference in Salt Lake City, Utah, in 2011. I love being able to share my knowledge and projects with my readers. I've met some amazing people through the online sewing community, and I'm so thankful to be a part of it.

2. Sew the gray strips together end to end to make a long strip. Measure the length of the quilt top. Trim the two gray strips to this length and sew them to the sides of the quilt top. Press the seam allowances toward the border. Measure the width of the quilt top and trim two gray strips to this measurement. Sew these strips to the top and bottom of the quilt top; press.

FINISHING THE QUILT

For free, downloadable, illustrated how-to instructions on any finishing techniques, go to ShopMartingale.com/HowtoQuilt.

1. Layer the quilt top, batting, and backing; baste the layers together. Quilt as desired.

2. Bind the quilt using the yellow binding strips. Add a label.

❝ | Optional Pieced Backing

From the leftover yellow, aqua, teal, and dark-gray fabrics, cut 29 rectangles, 2½" x 18½". Randomly sew the strips together along their long edges to make a pieced strip. Cut a 57"-long piece of fabric in half lengthwise to make two 20" x 57" pieces. Sew the 57"-long pieces on opposite sides of the pieced strip to complete the quilt back.

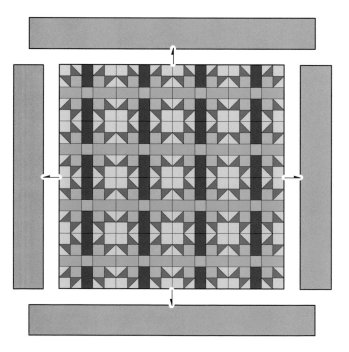

A SHIFT IN PERSPECTIVE

Designed and made by
John Q. Adams

FINISHED QUILT: 82½" x 88½"

This modern quilt, a variation of a simple strip quilt made from squares, rectangles, and triangles, creates an interesting visual effect that evokes movement (or shifting) due to the deliberate placement of its prints and colors. I designed this quilt both to showcase large prints and to emphasize a favorite color and pattern combination. As I was drawing plans for this quilt, it also seemed to represent a somewhat abstract interpretation of a tree trunk.

MATERIALS

Yardage is based on 42"-wide fabric.

Because long continuous strips, cut from the lengthwise grain, are required for this quilt, more yardage is required than you'll actually use when piecing the quilt top. If you're using a favorite color or print, there should be plenty of leftover fabric for additional projects—either another quilt, or maybe some coordinating pillows or shams. Another suggestion is to use the leftover fabrics to make a pieced back instead of purchasing backing fabric. If you prefer a more efficient use of fabric, you can use strips cut across the grain of the fabric and piece the long strips, which will require less yardage.

You'll need 10 fabrics for the quilt top, arranged in order from A to J.

2⅛ yards of fabric A
1¾ yards of fabric B
1¾ yards of fabric C
1⅝ yards of fabric D
1⅛ yards of fabric E
1⅝ yards of fabric F
2 yards of fabric G
2 yards of fabric H
½ yard of fabric I
½ yard of fabric J
¾ yard of dark print for binding
7½ yards of fabric for backing
88" x 94" piece of batting

CUTTING

If using directional prints, be sure to refer to the quilt assembly diagram on page 44 before making any cuts, especially when cutting a square in half diagonally. This will ensure that your pieces can be placed in such a way as to keep the orientation of the print intact.

From fabric A, cut:
1 strip, 6½" x 68½" (A1)
1 square, 13" x 13"; cut in half diagonally to yield 2 triangles (A2, A3)
1 strip, 6½" x 20½" (A4)

From the *lengthwise grain* of fabric B, cut:
1 strip, 12½" x 56½" (B1)
1 square, 13" x 13"; cut in half diagonally to yield 2 triangles (B2, B3)
1 strip, 12½" x 20½" (B4)

Continued on page 43

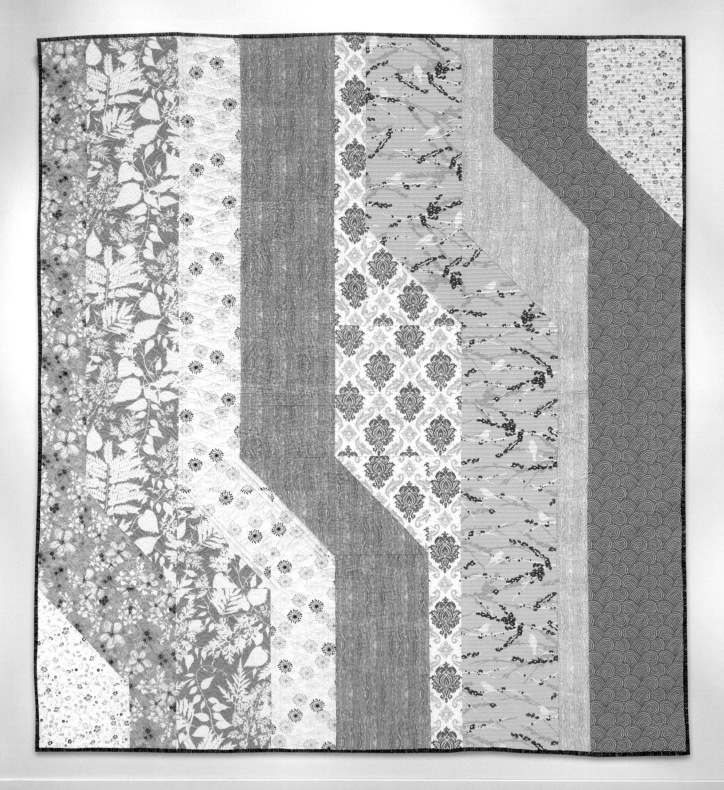

From the *lengthwise grain* of fabric C, cut:

1 strip, 8½" x 56½" (C1)

1 square, 13" x 13"; cut in half diagonally to yield
2 triangles (C2; 1 triangle is extra)

1 square, 5" x 5"; cut in half diagonally to yield
2 triangles (C3; 1 triangle is extra)

1 square, 9" x 9"; cut in half diagonally to yield
2 triangles (C4; 1 triangle is extra)

1 strip, 8½" x 24½" (C5)

From the *lengthwise grain* of fabric D, cut:

1 strip, 12½" x 52½" (D1)

1 square, 5" x 5"; cut in half diagonally to yield
2 triangles (D2; 1 triangle is extra)

1 rectangle, 4½" x 8½" (D3)

1 square, 9" x 9"; cut in half diagonally to yield
2 triangles (D4; 1 triangle is extra)

1 square, 13" x 13"; cut in half diagonally to yield
2 triangles (D5; 1 triangle is extra)

1 strip, 12½" x 24½" (D6)

From fabric E, cut:

2 strips, 4½" x 36½" (E1, E5)

1 square, 13" x 13"; cut in half diagonally to yield
2 triangles (E2, E3)

1 square, 16½" x 16½" (E4)

From the *lengthwise grain* of fabric F, cut:

1 strip, 12½" x 24½" (F1)

1 square, 13" x 13"; cut in half diagonally to yield
2 triangles (F2, F3)

1 strip, 12½" x 52½" (F4)

From the *lengthwise grain* of fabric G, cut:

1 strip, 4½" x 24½" (G1)

1 square, 13" x 13"; cut in half diagonally to yield
2 triangles (G2, G3)

1 strip, 4½" x 64½" (G4)

From the *lengthwise grain* of fabric H, cut:

1 square, 12½" x 12½" (H1)

1 square, 13" x 13"; cut in half diagonally to yield
2 triangles (H2, H3)

1 strip, 12½" x 64½" (H4)

From fabric I, cut:

1 square, 12½" x 12½" (I1)

1 square, 13" x 13"; cut in half diagonally to yield
2 triangles (I2; 1 triangle is extra)

From fabric J, cut:

1 square, 13" x 13"; cut in half diagonally to yield
2 triangles (J1; 1 triangle is extra)

1 rectangle, 8½" x 12½" (J2)

From the dark print, cut:

9 binding strips, 2½" x 42"

QUILT ASSEMBLY

This quilt is easily assembled in five vertical rows. Before starting to sew, I recommend laying out all the pieces on the floor or on your design wall according to the assembly diagram on page 44. After sewing each seam, return the completed unit or row to its correct position in the quilt layout.

1. Sew the A2 and J1 triangles together along their long edges to make a half-square-triangle unit. Press the seam allowances to one side (or press them open). Trim the unit to measure 12½" x 12½".

2. Repeat step 1 to make half-square-triangle units for each color combination as follows:

- Join A3 and B2 triangles. Trim to 12½" x 12½".
- Join B3 and C2 triangles. Trim to 12½" x 12½".
- Join C3 and D2 triangles. Trim to 4½" x 4½".
- Join C4 and D4 triangles. Trim to 8½" x 8½".
- Join D5 and E3 triangles. Trim to 12½" x 12½".
- Join E2 and F2 triangles. Trim to 12½" x 12½".
- Join F3 and G3 triangles. Trim to 12½" x 12½".
- Join G2 and H2 triangles. Trim to 12½" x 12½".
- Join H3 and I2 triangles. Trim to 12½" x 12½".

3. For row 1, sew the A3/B2 unit to the bottom edge of the B1 strip. Then sew the A1 strip to the left edge of the strip to make the top section. Sew the J1/A2 unit to the J2 rectangle; then add the A4 strip to the right edge to make the bottom section. Join the two sections to complete row 1. Press the seam allowances in the directions indicated by the arrows.

4. For row 2, sew the C3/D2 unit to the D3 rectangle. Then add the D1 strip to the top edge. Sew the C1 strip to the left edge to make the top section. Join the B3/C2 unit to the B4 strip. Join the C4/D4 unit to the C5 strip. Join the two strips to make the bottom section. Join the two sections to complete row 2. Press the seam allowances in the directions indicated by the arrows.

5. For row 3, sew the E2/F2 unit to the F1 strip. Then add the E1 strip to the left edge and the E4 square to the bottom edge to make the top section. Join the D5/E3 unit to the D6 strip. Then add the

E5 strip to make the bottom section. Join the two sections to complete row 3. Press the seam allowances in the directions indicated by the arrows.

6. For row 4, sew the G2/H2 unit to the H1 square; add the G1 strip to make the top section. Sew the F3/G3 unit to the F4 strip; then add the G4 strip to make the bottom section. Join the two sections to complete row 4. Press the seam allowances in the directions indicated by the arrows.

7. For row 5, sew the H3/I2 unit to the I1 square; add the H4 strip to the bottom edge to complete the row; press.

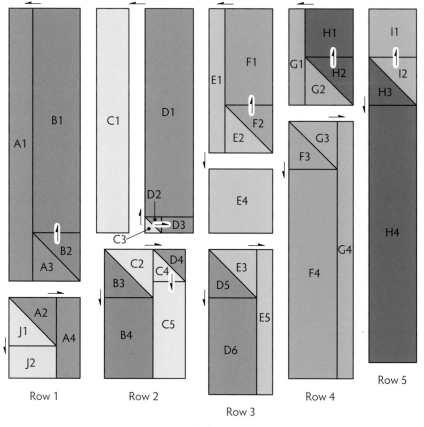

Quilt assembly

8. Join the five vertical rows to complete the quilt top. Press the seam allowances open.

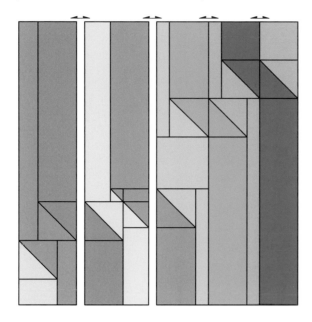

FINISHING THE QUILT

For free, downloadable, illustrated how-to instructions on any finishing techniques, go to ShopMartingale.com/HowtoQuilt.

1. Layer the quilt top, batting, and backing; baste the layers together. Quilt as desired.

2. Bind the quilt using the dark-print binding strips. Add a label.

Designer Bio
JOHN Q. ADAMS
QuiltDad.com

I'm a husband and a father of three who enjoys sewing and quilting in my spare time. I was born and raised in Brooklyn, New York, and currently live in Holly Springs, North Carolina, with my wife, Kiely; twin daughters, Megan and Bevin; and son, Sean. I earned my undergraduate and master's degrees at the University of North Carolina at Chapel Hill and, when I'm not sewing, I enjoy cheering for the UNC Tar Heels.

Inspired by the growing number of crafting blogs and the emergence of vibrant, modern fabrics in the textile industry, I convinced my wife to teach me how to use her sewing machine in 2004 and haven't looked back. I started my popular blog, QuiltDad.com, in 2008 as a way to share my love of patchwork with others.

Since then, I have become very active in online quilting communities. Today, I apply my modern quilting aesthetic by designing quilt patterns for both fabric designers and companies, and contributing frequently to creative blogs, books, and other collaborative endeavors. I'm also a cofounder of the eMagazine *Fat Quarterly*.

45

SILO

Designed and made by
Heather Jones

FINISHED QUILT: 62½" x 67½"

✳ This quilt was inspired by a large metal silo that's about 10 miles from my house. The quilt was chosen as a winner by Denyse Schmidt in the "Find Your Own Voice" challenge, part of the Modern Quilt Guild's Project Modern in 2011. "Silo" is truly a reflection of my voice as a modern quilter.

MATERIALS

Yardage is based on 42"-wide fabric.

2¾ yards of cream solid for blocks and binding*
2¼ yards of blue solid for blocks*
½ yard of gray solid for sashing*
4 yards of fabric for backing**
68" x 73" piece of batting

Heather used Moda Fabrics in the following solid colors: Blue Raspberry (blue) and Bella Natural (cream). She also used Robert Kaufman Kona Cotton in the color Stone (gray).

**Or see "Optional Pieced Backing" on page 49.*

CUTTING

From the blue solid, cut:
16 strips, 4½" x 42"

From the cream solid, cut:
16 strips, 4½" x 42"
7 binding strips, 2½" x 42"

From the gray solid, cut:
9 strips, 1½" x 42"; cut *4 of the strips* into 8 strips, 1½" x 16½"

BLOCK ASSEMBLY

1. Join blue and cream 4½"-wide strips along one long edge to make a strip set. Press the seam allowances open. Make 16.

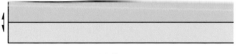

Make 16.

2. Sew two strip sets from step 1 together as shown to make a 16½"-wide strip set. Press the seam allowances open. Make eight of these strip sets.

Make 8.

3. Trim the selvages from one end of each strip set. Crosscut one 24½"-wide segment from each strip set. Label these segments A blocks. Then crosscut the remainder of the strip sets into four 12½"-wide segments and label them B blocks.

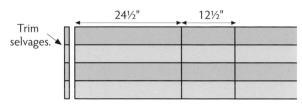

Cut 8 segments, 24½" wide (A blocks),
and 4 segments, 12½" wide (B blocks).

❝ | Orientation of Blocks

Notice the orientation of the A blocks as you are constructing your quilt top. Half of them will be set with the blue strip at the top and the other half of them will be set with the cream strip at the top. This is done simply by turning the blocks upside down.

ROW ASSEMBLY

Refer to the assembly diagram on page 49 and the photo on page 46 for placement guidance.

Rows 1 and 3

1. Position an A block with the blue strip on top and sew a gray 1½" x 16½" strip to the right end of the block. Press the seam allowances open.

2. Position an A block with the cream strip on top and sew a gray 1½" x 16½" strip to the right end of the block. Press the seam allowances open.

3. Join the pieced sections from steps 1 and 2. Press the seam allowances open.

4. With the blue strip on top, sew a B block to the end of the row to complete row 1. Press the seam allowances open. The row should measure 62½" long.

5. Repeat steps 1–4 to make row 3.

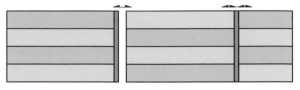

Make 2.

Rows 2 and 4

1. Position a B block with the blue strip on top and sew a gray 1½" x 16½" strip to the right end of the block. Press the seam allowances open.

2. Position an A block with the cream strip on top and sew a gray 1½" x 16½" strip to the right end of the block. Press the seam allowances open.

3. Join the pieced sections from steps 1 and 2. Press the seam allowances open.

4. With the blue strip on top, sew an A block to the end of the row to complete row 2. Press the seam allowances open. The row should measure 62½" long.

5. Repeat steps 1–4 to make row 4.

Make 2.

QUILT ASSEMBLY

1. Sew the five remaining gray 1½" x 42" strips together end to end to make a long strip and then cut three 62½"-long sashing strips.

2. Lay out the four rows as shown in the assembly diagram, placing the gray sashing strips between the rows.

3. Join the rows and sashing strips. Press the seam allowances open.

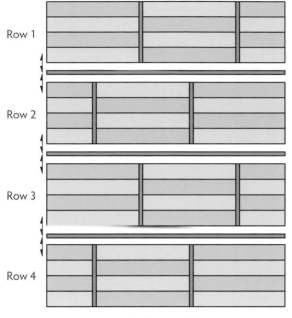

Row 1

Row 2

Row 3

Row 4

Quilt assembly

FINISHING THE QUILT

For free, downloadable, illustrated how-to instructions on any finishing techniques, go to ShopMartingale.com/HowtoQuilt.

1. Layer the quilt top, batting, and backing; baste the layers together. Quilt as desired.

2. Bind the quilt using the cream binding strips. Add a label.

❝ | Optional Pieced Backing

I used leftover strips and block pieces from the construction of the front to make an improvisational, scrappy back.

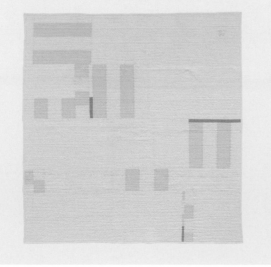

Designer Bio
HEATHER JONES
OliveAndOllie.com

I'm a designer, seamstress, and modern quilter. I live in Cincinnati with my husband, Jeff, and two young children, Aidan and Olivia, who are my biggest supporters as well as my greatest sources of inspiration. I'm also the founder and former president of the Cincinnati Modern Quilt Guild and I'm working on my first line of appliqué, sewing, and quilting patterns.

I have great respect for the art of quilt-making and I love to bring a modern twist to traditional patterns. I'm often inspired by everyday places and things that many people wouldn't even notice, and I'm always excited by the challenge to translate that inspiration into my work. Three of my original quilts were chosen as winners of the Modern Quilt Guild's Project Modern challenges, a year-long national quilting competition.

I've had a blog for over four years, but I only recently began to devote time to blogging regularly—at least three or four times per week. It's fun to share my life and work with so many other people.

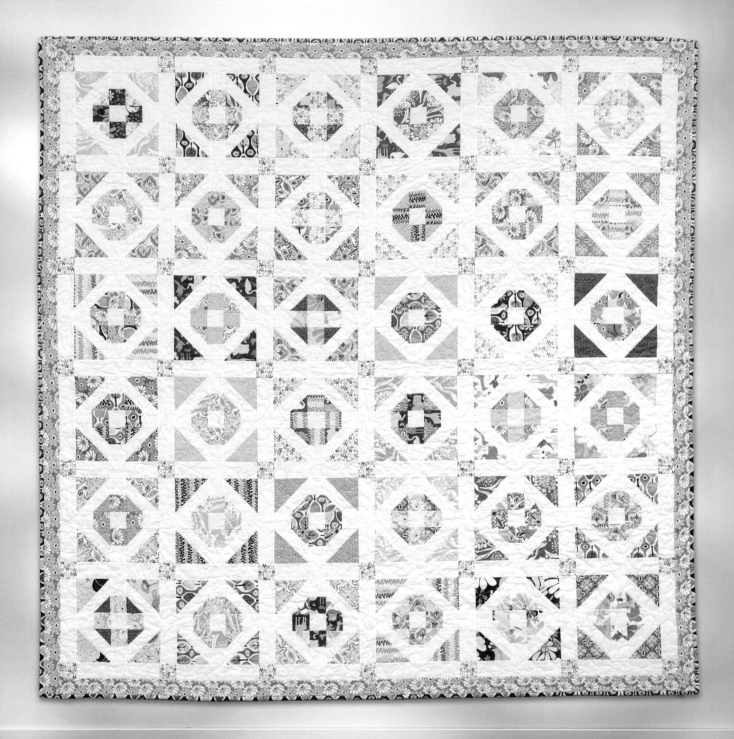

DIAMOND CROSSES

Designed and made by Kate Henderson

FINISHED QUILT: 78½" x 78½"
FINISHED BLOCKS: 10" x 10"

✳ I love to see what quilt blocks and shapes I can make from 10" precut squares. This block incorporates two of my favorite shapes—diamonds and crosses. Choosing three high-contrast fabrics for each block will make the design pop.

MATERIALS

Yardage is based on 42"-wide fabric.

4 yards of cream fabric for blocks and sashing

36 assorted 10" squares for blocks

⅔ yard of blue floral for border

⅜ yard of blue print for sashing squares

¾ yard of multicolored print for binding

7 yards of fabric for backing*

84" x 84" piece of batting

*If the backing fabric measures a true 42" wide after trimming off the selvages, you'll only need 4¾ yards of fabric for backing.

CUTTING

From the cream fabric, cut:
9 strips, 5" x 42"; cut into 72 squares, 5" x 5"
34 strips, 2½" x 42"; cut into:
    84 rectangles, 2½" x 10½"
    180 squares, 2½" x 2½"

From *each* of the assorted 10" squares, cut:*
2 squares, 5" x 5" (72 total)
8 squares, 2½" x 2½" (288 total)

From the blue print, cut:
4 strips, 2½" x 42"; cut into 49 squares, 2½" x 2½"

From the blue floral, cut:
8 strips, 2½" x 42"

From the multicolored print, cut:
9 binding strips, 2½" x 42"

*Refer to cutting diagram.

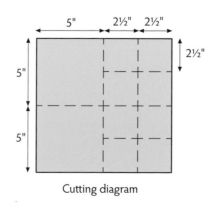

Cutting diagram

BLOCK ASSEMBLY

For each block, you'll need the following pieces:
Cream: two 5" squares and five 2½" squares
Three *different* assorted squares: two matching 5" squares, four matching 2½" squares, and four matching 2½" squares

1. Mark a diagonal line on the wrong side of a cream 5" square. Layer the marked square with an assorted 5" square, right sides together, and stitch ¼" on each side of the marked line. Cut the squares apart on the line to make two half-square-triangle units. Press the seam allowances toward the darker triangle. Trim the units to measure 4½" x 4½". Repeat to make four matching half-square-triangle units total.

Make 4.

2. Draw a diagonal line on the wrong side of four matching assorted 2½" squares. Place a square on the cream corner of a half-square-triangle unit, right sides together. Sew on the marked line. Trim the excess corner fabric leaving a ¼" seam allowance. Press the seam allowances toward the resulting triangle. Make four matching units.

3. Sew a cream 2½" square to an assorted 2½" square. Press the seam allowances toward the darker square. Make four matching units.

Make 4.

4. Lay out the units from steps 2 and 3 in three rows as shown. Place the remaining cream 2½" square in the center of the block. Join the pieces in each row. Press the seam allowances in the directions indicated by the arrows.

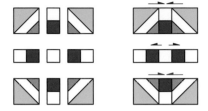

5. Join the rows and press the seam allowances toward the center. Repeat the process to make 36 blocks total.

Make 36.

QUILT ASSEMBLY

1. Sew six blocks and seven cream rectangles together, alternating them as shown. Press the seam allowances toward the cream rectangles. Make six block rows.

Make 6.

2. Sew six cream rectangles and seven blue squares together, alternating them as shown. Press the seam allowances toward the cream rectangles. Make seven sashing rows.

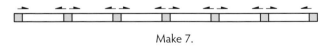

Make 7.

3. Referring to the diagram on page 53 and the photo on page 50, lay out the block rows and sashing rows in a pleasing arrangement. Join the rows and press the seam allowances toward the sashing rows.

4. Sew the blue floral strips together in pairs to make four long strips. Measure the length of the quilt top. Trim two of the strips to this length and sew them to the sides of the quilt top. Press the seam allowances toward the border. Measure the width of the quilt top and trim the two remaining strips to this measurement. Sew these strips to the top and bottom of the quilt top; press.

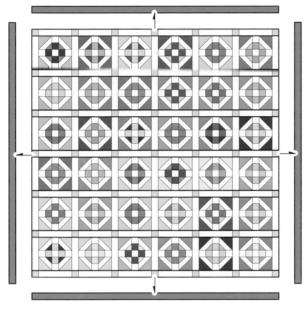

Quilt assembly

FINISHING THE QUILT

For free, downloadable, illustrated how-to instructions on any finishing techniques, go to ShopMartingale.com/HowtoQuilt.

1. Layer the quilt top, batting, and backing; baste the layers together. Quilt as desired.

2. Bind the quilt using the multicolored binding strips. Add a label.

Designer Bio
KATE HENDERSON
TwoLittleBanshees.com

The first time I used a sewing machine, I was 12 and I made a pair of shorts. I've sewn clothes for myself ever since. When I was 16, I saw a quilting magazine and made my first quilt—a Log Cabin. It took forever as all the pieces were cut with scissors, so that first quilt was also my last quilt for a few years.

I started quilting again while teaching in a remote community in Australia. There were no quilting shops for hundreds of kilometers, so I would have kits sent to me. After moving to a small town in the south of Western Australia and giving birth to twins, I discovered craft blogs on the Internet. It was like I had found my people. This connection probably saved me from going crazy being home with two babies.

Through blogs, my eyes were opened to new fabrics, colors, designs, and techniques. But my favorite quilts are those made with scraps from the clothes and soft toys I sew for myself and my children—my girls love to identify the fabrics that way.

Being a self-taught sewist and quilter means I haven't had any rules to follow. I simply make things that I like and that my family likes. I find the best test of a quilt is how much it's used and whether we need a roster for whose turn it is to sleep with it.

EVERYTHING'S COMING UP RAINBOWS

Designed and made by
Krista Fleckenstein

FINISHED QUILT: 70" x 90"
FINISHED BLOCKS: 14" x 14"

✳ I created the original version of this quilt as a mini wall hanging for a Flickr swap. My partner loves rainbows and using all of the colors against the light-gray background really made them pop. Even in this larger bed-sized quilt, this pattern is a great way to use small pieces of your favorite prints. Or try using various shades of solids.

MATERIALS

Yardage is based on 42"-wide fabric. Fat eighths measure 9" x 21".

4⅞ yards of light-gray solid for blocks and border
1¼ yards of white solid for blocks
1 fat eighth *each* of 4 assorted red prints for blocks
1 fat eighth *each* of 4 assorted orange prints for blocks
1 fat eighth *each* of 4 assorted yellow prints for blocks
1 fat eighth *each* of 4 assorted green prints for blocks
1 fat eighth *each* of 4 assorted blue prints for blocks
1 fat eighth *each* of 4 assorted purple prints for blocks
¾ yard of dark print for binding
5½ yards of fabric for backing
76" x 96" piece of batting

CUTTING

Divide the assorted prints into two sets; each set will have *two each* of the red, orange, yellow, green, blue, and purple prints. Label the sets A and B.

From *each* of the set A prints, cut:
1 square, 9" x 9" (12 total)

From *each* of the set B prints, cut:
1 square, 8" x 8" (12 total)

From the white solid, cut:
24 rectangles, 1½" x 9"
24 rectangles, 1½" x 11"
24 rectangles, 1½" x 8"
24 rectangles, 1½" x 10"

From the *lengthwise grain* of the light-gray solid, cut:
4 strips, 7½" x 42½"

From the remainder of the light-gray solid, cut:
24 rectangles, 2½" x 11"
24 rectangles, 2½" x 15"
24 rectangles, 3" x 10"
24 rectangles, 3" x 15"
4 strips, 3½" x 35½"

From the dark print, cut:
8 binding strips, 2½" x 42"

BLOCK ASSEMBLY

The blocks are made in two sets, A and B, using the designated group of fabrics for each set.

Set A

1. Sew white 1½" x 9" rectangles to opposite sides of an assorted 9" square. Press the seam allowances toward the rectangles.

2. Sew white 1½" x 11" rectangles to the two remaining sides of the assorted square. Press the seam allowances toward the rectangles.

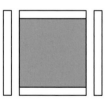

3. Sew light-gray 2½" x 11" rectangles to opposite sides of the square from step 2. Sew light-gray 2½" x 15" rectangles to the two remaining sides of the square to complete the block. Press the seam allowances toward the newly added rectangles. The block should measure 15" x 15". Repeat the process to make 12 blocks total.

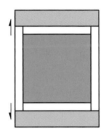

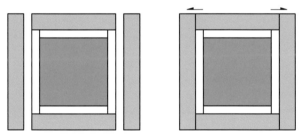

Make 12.

Set B

1. Sew white 1½" x 8" rectangles to opposite sides of an assorted 8" square. Press the seam allowances toward the rectangles.

2. Sew white 1½" x 10" rectangles to the two remaining sides of the assorted square. Press the seam allowances toward the rectangles.

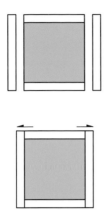

3. Sew light-gray 3" x 10" rectangles to opposite sides of the square from step 2. Sew light-gray 3" x 15" rectangles to thc two remaining sides of the square to complete the block. Press the seam allowances toward the newly added rectangles. The block should measure 15" x 15". Repeat the process to make 12 blocks total.

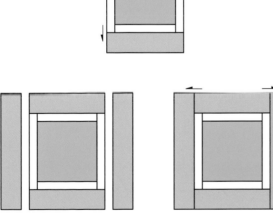

Make 12.

FINAL BLOCK ASSEMBLY

1. Cut each of the set A blocks in half horizontally and vertically as shown to make four quarter blocks. The blocks should measure 7½" x 7½". Make 48 quarter blocks, keeping like fabrics together.

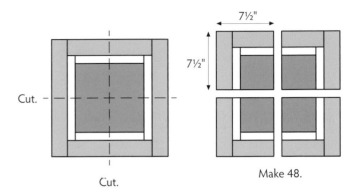

Make 48.

2. Repeat step 1, using the set B blocks to make 48 quarter blocks, keeping like fabrics togcther.

3. Lay out two different A quarter blocks and two different B quarter blocks from the same color family as shown. Sew the quarter blocks together in pairs and press the seam allowances to one side. Join the pairs; press. The block should measure 14½" x 14½".

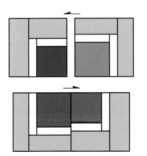
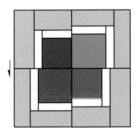

4. Repeat step 3 with the remaining quarter blocks to make 24 blocks total. You should have four blocks each from the red, orange, yellow, green, blue, and purple prints.

QUILT ASSEMBLY

1. Referring to the assembly diagram for color placement, arrange the blocks in six rows of four blocks each. Sew the blocks together in rows. Press the seam allowances in opposite directions from row to row.

2. Join the rows. Press the seam allowances in one direction. The quilt top should measure 56½" x 84½".

3. Join the light-gray 7½" x 42½" strips in pairs to make two 84½"-long strips. Sew these strips to opposite sides of the quilt top. Press the seam allowances toward the border.

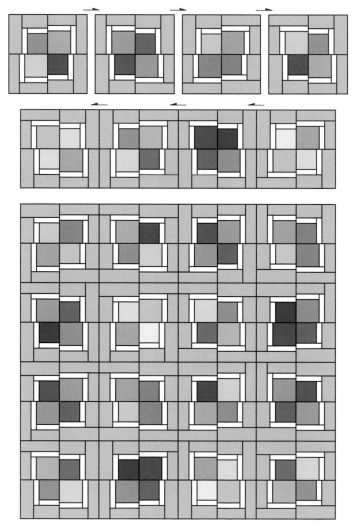

Quilt assembly

4. Join the light-gray 3½" x 35½" strips in pairs to make two 70½"-long strips. Sew these strips to the top and bottom of the quilt top to complete the outer border. Press the seam allowances toward the border.

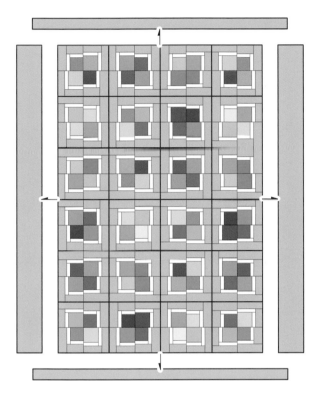

FINISHING THE QUILT

For free, downloadable, illustrated how-to instructions on any finishing techniques, go to ShopMartingale.com/HowtoQuilt.

1. Layer the quilt top, batting, and backing; baste the layers together. Quilt as desired.

2. Bind the quilt using the dark-print binding strips. Add a label.

Designer Bio

KRISTA FLECKENSTEIN

SpottedStone.blogspot.com

I live and create in Anchorage, Alaska, with my husband, children, and two dogs. When I was growing up, my mom and her sisters were prolific quilters, and I was always surrounded by piles of fabric and the hum of a sewing machine. But it wasn't until I became an adult and had children of my own that I started sewing. I began making simple baby quilts for friends, and before I knew it, I was hooked.

When I started my blog in 2010, I had no idea it would become such a fulfilling part of my life. My switch from working full time to being a stay-at-home mom after my son was born brought insecurities about how I would continue to connect with others. Through blogging and participation in the quilting community on Flickr, I've found so much inspiration, met incredible friends, and have been challenged to push my creativity. It's also enabled me to find my own style. Hundreds of posts later, I still find myself excited to blog and share my work with others.

It's been rewarding to be a part of the growing modern quilting movement as well. Modern quilters are doing their own thing—exploring fabric combinations that make them feel good, supporting each other as they learn new skills, and pushing the limits of design. The more excited we get about quilting, the better!

RAINBOW STASH BUSTER

Designed and pieced by
Megan Jimenez;
quilted by Wendy Castle

FINISHED QUILT: 54½" x 54½"
FINISHED BLOCKS: 13½" x 13½"

✳ I love making stash-buster quilts, and I think most quilters do too. In this quilt, I used scraps of some of my favorite prints. But you don't have to make it in rainbow colors; make your quilt unique by using *your* favorite prints and colors.

MATERIALS

Yardage is based on 42"-wide fabric.

8 strips, 5½" x 42", of white fabric for blocks
7 strips, 5½" x 42", of assorted orange and yellow prints for blocks
6 strips, 5½" x 42", of assorted blue and green prints for blocks
4 strips, 5½" x 42", of assorted red and pink prints for blocks
3 strips, 5½" x 42", of assorted purple prints for blocks
½ yard of purple print for binding
3½ yards of fabric for backing*
60" x 60" piece of batting

*Or see "Optional Pieced Backing" on page 63.

CUTTING

From the white strips, cut:
50 squares, 5½" x 5½"

From *each* of the orange and yellow strips, cut:
6 squares, 5½" x 5½" (42 total; 2 are extra)

From *each* of the blue and green strips, cut:
6 squares, 5½" x 5½" (36 total; 4 are extra)

From *each* of the red and pink strips, cut:
4 squares, 5½" x 5½" (16 total)

From *each* of the purple strips, cut:
2 squares, 5½" x 5½" (6 total)

From the purple print, cut:
6 binding strips, 2½" x 42"

BLOCK ASSEMBLY

1. Mark a diagonal line on the wrong side of a white square. Layer the marked square with an orange or yellow square, right sides together, and stitch ¼" on each side of the marked line. Cut the squares apart on the line to make two half-square-triangle units. Press the seam allowances toward the darker triangle. Trim the units to measure 5" x 5". Make 40 units total.

Make 40.

2. Repeat step 1 to make the number of half-square-triangle units indicated for each color combination:

- Pair orange or yellow squares with different orange or yellow squares to make 20 units.
- Pair blue or green squares with white squares to make 32 units.
- Pair blue or green squares with different blue or green squares to make 16 units.
- Pair red or pink squares with white squares to make 16 units.
- Pair red or pink squares with different red or pink squares to make 8 units.
- Pair purple squares with white squares to make 12 units.

3. Referring to the photo on page 60 and the block diagrams, lay out nine half-square-triangle units as shown. Sew the units together in rows. Press the seam allowances in the directions indicated by the arrows. Join the rows; press. Make the number of blocks indicated for each color combination.

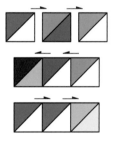

Block A.
Make 4.

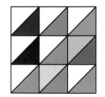

Block B.
Make 4.

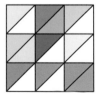

Block C.
Make 8.

QUILT ASSEMBLY

1. Lay out one A block, one B block, and two C blocks as shown. Sew the blocks together in pairs. Press the seam allowances in the directions indicated by the arrows. Sew the pairs together to make a quadrant. Press the seam allowances to one side. Repeat to make four quadrants total.

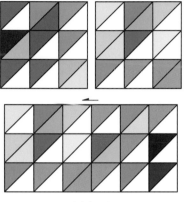

Make 4.

2. Lay out the quadrants from step 1 as shown. Sew the quadrants together in rows and then join the rows. Press the seam allowances in the directions indicated by the arrows.

Quilt assembly

FINISHING THE QUILT

For free, downloadable, illustrated how-to instructions on any finishing techniques, go to ShopMartingale.com/HowtoQuilt.

1. Layer the quilt top, batting, and backing; baste the layers together. Quilt as desired.

2. Bind the quilt using the purple binding strips. Add a label.

❝ | Optional Pieced Backing

To make the optional pieced backing, you'll need two 7½" x 42" strips *each* of seven different assorted prints and three 6" x 42" strips *each* of a gray or neutral print.

1. Sew like-print strips together end to end; then trim the long strip to measure 60" long. Make seven 60"-long strips.

2. Join the neutral strips end to end and then cut two 60"-long strips.

3. Sew the assorted-print strips and neutral strips together along their long edges, beginning and ending with a neutral strip. Press the seam allowances open.

Designer Bio
MEGAN JIMENEZ
QuiltStory.blogspot.com

I'm the youngest of seven children and learned to sew as a little girl. I have always loved to sew and make things by hand, which led me into a very modern and darling quilt shop. The moment I walked into the shop, I was hooked and knew I had to make a quilt for my first baby who was due in a couple of months. I now live in Arizona with my amazing husband; my sons, Sawyer and Oliver; my baby girl; and my fabric.

My sister, Heather, and I design quilt patterns, offered through our company, Quilt Story. In May 2010, we started our blog by the same name. We feature our own projects, other quilters, tutorials, and other fun series and events. I absolutely love the community we've found online, with so many kind and helpful people. Above all I find blogging inspiring—seeing everyone's projects makes me want to hop on the machine.

To me, modern quilting means so many things: simple quilts; taking a block that is considered traditional, adding new fabric lines and a new layout; incorporating solid fabrics into a design; off-set or wonky blocks; and more! I try not to get too wrapped up in labeling quilts as modern or otherwise, but more in whatever emotions a quilt makes me feel—and hopefully those are happy, excited, and giddy.

PETAL POD

Designed and made by
Jessica Kovach

FINISHED QUILT: 63½" x 80½"
FINISHED BLOCKS: 6" x 9"

✳ Adding a few simple curved seams in your quilt takes this modern quilt design from ordinary to extraordinary.

MATERIALS

Yardage is based on 42"-wide fabric.

4¼ yards of gray print for background and binding
⅛ yard *each* of 21 assorted prints for petal pods
5 yards of fabric for backing
69" x 86" piece of batting
Template plastic

CUTTING

Patterns for A and B are on page 67. Make a plastic template of each.

From *each* of the assorted prints, cut:
2 squares, 3½" x 3½" (42 total)
1 rectangle, 3½" x 6½" (21 total)
2 of template A (42 total)

From the *lengthwise grain* of the gray print, cut:
1 strip, 42" x 63½"
1 strip, 23" x 63½"
5 binding strips, 2½" x 63½"

From the remaining gray print, cut:
2 strips, 5" x 42"; cut into 21 rectangles, 3½" x 5"

BLOCK ASSEMBLY

1. Align the straight edges of template B with the raw edges of a gray rectangle and trace the template as shown. Each rectangle will yield two B pieces.

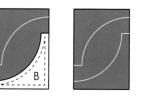

2. Use scissors to cut out the B pieces on the traced line. Make 42 B pieces.

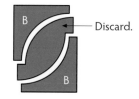

3. Fold an A piece and a B piece in half along the curved edge and finger-press to mark the center line. With right sides together and piece B on top, match and pin the center marks and ends. Pin along the curve, easing the fabric as needed.

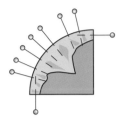

> **❝ | Making a Smooth Curve**
>
> Make ⅛" snips in the curved seam allowance of piece B to help ease the fabric.

4. Join the pieces using a ¼" seam allowance. Press the seam allowances toward the B piece. Make two matching units for each block (42 total).

Make 2 for each
block (42 total).

5. Lay out two assorted squares, one assorted rectangle, and two units from step 4, all matching, as shown. Sew each curved unit to a square to make a rectangle. Press the seam allowances toward the square. Then sew the rectangles together to complete the block. Press the seam allowances toward the center. Repeat to make 21 blocks total.

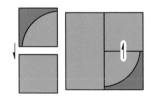 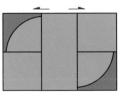

Make 21.

QUILT ASSEMBLY

1. Arrange the blocks in three rows of seven blocks each. Sew the blocks together in rows, pressing the seam allowances in alternating directions from row to row. Join the rows. Press the seam allowances in the same direction. The pieced section should measure 18½" x 63½".

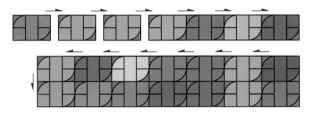

2. Sew the gray 42" x 63½" strip to the top of the pieced section. Press the seam allowances toward the gray rectangle.

3. Sew the gray 23" x 63½" strip to the bottom of the pieced section to complete the quilt top. Press the seam allowances toward the gray rectangle. Trim the quilt top as needed to measure 63½" x 80½".

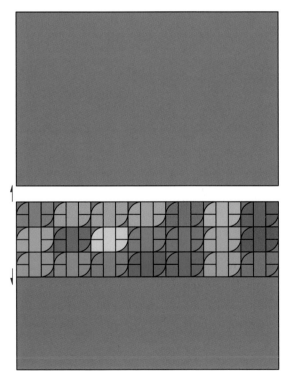

Quilt assembly

FINISHING THE QUILT

For free, downloadable, illustrated how-to instructions on any finishing techniques, go to ShopMartingale.com/HowtoQuilt.

1. Layer the quilt top, batting, and backing; baste the layers together. Quilt as desired.

2. Bind the quilt using the gray binding strips. Add a label.

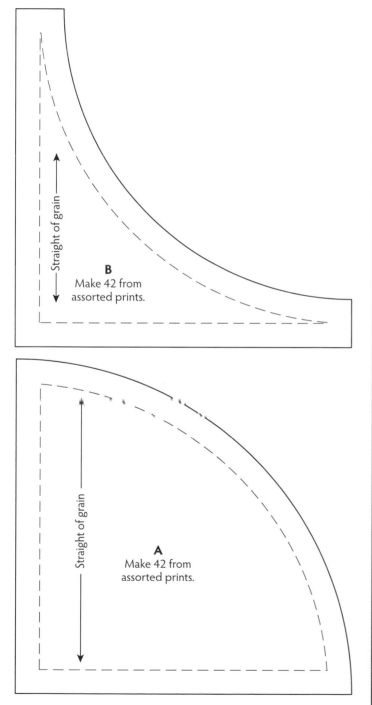

Designer Bio
JESSICA KOVACH
TwinFibers.blogspot.com

As a stay-at-home mom of three, sewing and quilting have been great creative outlets for me. My sister and I started a blog a few years ago as a way to keep track of the things we sew, and to keep us motivated to finish projects. Along the way, I've been able to participate in many quilting bees, swaps, and books, which always inspire me to try a new technique or something I've thought up.

Being creative with my sewing and learning new techniques have provided me with much happiness and my hope is that I inspire others to do the same. I'm always surprised when someone thinks I'm a "modern quilter." I really like vintage patterns, colors, and fabrics, and those aren't things I would call modern. But, I do like defined repetition in my quilt designs and maybe that's what makes my quilting modern.

It's been so much fun to become friends with like-minded people through their blogs. I'm grateful for the opportunities and experiences I've had because of my blog and look forward to what is yet to come. Please visit TwinFibers.blogspot.com if you'd like to see what I've been up to.

LIGHTNING STRIKES

Designed and pieced by Audrie Bidwell;
quilted by Laura McCarrick

FINISHED QUILT: 63" x 72"

⁎ I love 60°-triangle quilts and just how bold and graphic they can look. This design mimics lightning streaking across the quilt, and I used bright colors—and polka dots—to make it fun and lively.

MATERIALS

Yardage is based on 42"-wide fabric.

½ yard *each* of 6 assorted dark fabrics
½ yard *each* of 5 assorted light fabrics
½ yard of gray tone-on-tone fabric for background
⅔ yard of dark-gray solid for binding
4 yards of fabric for backing
69" x 78" piece of batting
60°-triangle ruler, at least 6" tall, or template plastic

CUTTING

From *each* of the assorted light and assorted dark fabrics, cut:
2 strips, 6½" x 42" (22 total)

From the gray tone-on-tone fabric, cut:
2 strips, 6½" x 42"

From the dark-gray solid, cut:
8 binding strips, 2½" x 42"

QUILT ASSEMBLY

Patterns for A and B are on page 70. Make a plastic template of each.

1. Open each 6½"-wide strip and use the triangle templates to cut triangles across the width of the fabric. From *each* fabric cut 17 A triangles, one B triangle, and one B reversed triangle.

2. On a design wall, arrange eight A triangles with the tip pointing down and place matching B and B reversed triangles at the ends. Then position nine A triangles with the tip pointing up to complete the row. Lay out each row as follows:

- Row 1: Gray points down and dark fabric #1 points up.
- Row 2: Dark fabric #1 points down and light fabric #1 points up.
- Row 3: Light fabric #1 points down and dark fabric #2 points up.
- Row 4: Dark fabric #2 points down and light fabric #2 points up.
- Row 5: Light fabric #2 points down and dark fabric #3 points up.
- Row 6: Dark fabric #3 points down and light fabric #3 points up.
- Row 7: Light fabric #3 points down and dark fabric #4 points up.
- Row 8: Dark fabric #4 points down and light fabric #4 points up.
- Row 9: Light fabric #4 points down and dark fabric #5 points up.
- Row 10: Dark fabric #5 points down and light fabric #5 points up.
- Row 11: Light fabric #5 points down and dark fabric #6 points up.
- Row 12: Dark fabric #6 points down and gray points up.

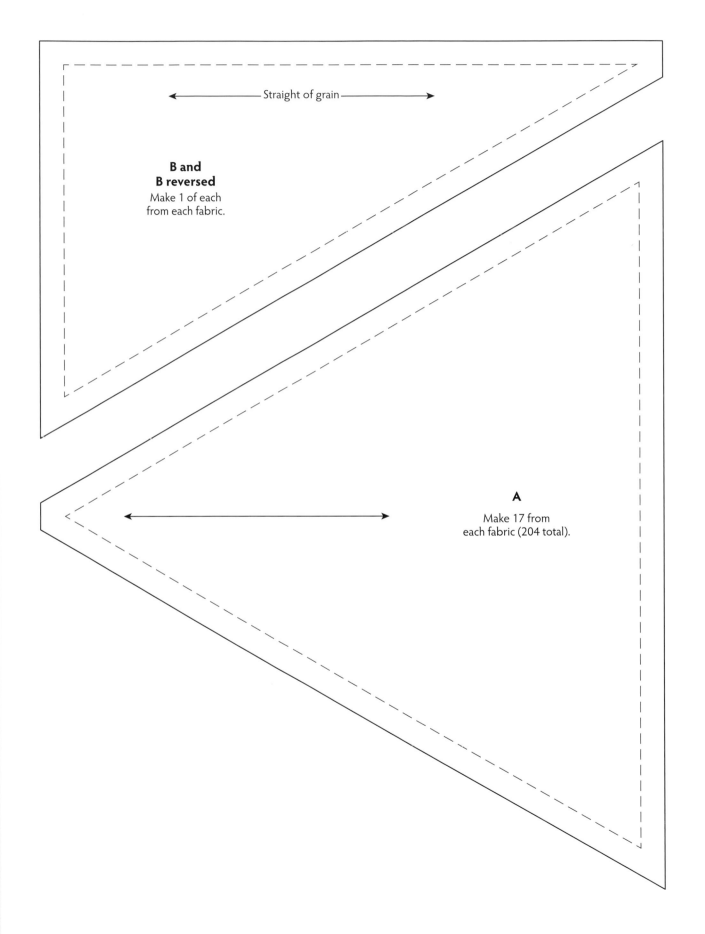

Straight of grain

**B and
B reversed**
Make 1 of each
from each fabric.

A
Make 17 from
each fabric (204 total).

« LIGHTNING STRIKES »

3. Sew the triangles in each row together, beginning and ending with a B triangle. Press all seam allowances open.

> ❝ | **Pressing**
>
> I recommend pressing your seam allowances open to reduce bulk where the seams meet.

4. Sew the rows together as shown, keeping the points centered and the side edges straight to complete the quilt top. Trim and square up the corners as needed.

Quilt assembly

FINISHING THE QUILT

For free, downloadable, illustrated how-to instructions on any finishing techniques, go to ShopMartingale.com/HowtoQuilt.

1. Layer the quilt top, batting, and backing; baste the layers together. Quilt as desired.

2. Bind the quilt using the dark-gray binding strips. Add a label.

Designer Bio
AUDRIE BIDWELL
BlueIsBleu.blogspot.com

I grew up in Singapore and Australia, and moved to the States a few years ago. I didn't know anyone in my new home, so I decided I needed something to do to avoid sheer boredom. I've always been a writer, so starting a blog seemed like a good idea. It was just going to be a place where I could share the things I love and covet, but it has become so much more.

Shortly after I started my blog, I got back into sewing and taught myself to quilt. I very quickly discovered that it was much more than just a hobby. I had found something I truly love and have a great passion for. And the icing on the cake is the many friends I've made in the online modern-quilting community.

I don't think I have a defined style, but I'm drawn to the bright colors and clean lines of modern quilting. Modern quilting means different things to different people and in my opinion, modern quilting couldn't exist without the foundation of traditional quilts. I like taking old ideas and making them fresh and new. I believe there are no rules when it comes to quilting, so I'm thankful I taught myself to quilt, free of any concept of what a quilt needs to be.

IMPROV COLOR BLOCKS

Designed and made by
Kati Spencer

FINISHED QUILT: 60½" x 70½"
FINISHED BLOCKS: 10" x 10"

✳ I'm a scrap saver. This is a great quilt to use up those favorite scraps. I find improvisational piecing a fun change from the precision required in traditional piecing.

MATERIALS

Yardage is based on 42"-wide fabric.

8 to 12 assorted scraps, 1" to 3" wide and 4" to 12" long, for each block (96 to 144 total)

3¼ yards of gray solid for blocks and border*

⅝ yard of dark print for binding

3⅔ yards of fabric for backing**

66" x 76" piece of batting

10½" square acrylic ruler

*After the selvages are trimmed off, the fabric needs to measure at least 42" wide for this project. If your fabric is narrower, you'll need a total of 4⅞ yards of gray solid.

** Or see "Optional Pieced Backing" on page 77.

> ❝ | **Fabric Tips**
>
> Choose solid and print fabrics—most anything bright and fun works. The fabrics in each individual block should be similar in color. Consider incorporating one or two contrasting scraps into the block to add interest. The contrasting color can easily be pulled from the colors in another scrap used in the block.
>
> Try fussy cutting a small section or design from a favorite fabric and building the block around that design.

CUTTING

From the *lengthwise grain* of the gray solid, cut:*
1 strip, 20½" x 60½"
1 strip, 20½" x 50½"

From the remaining gray solid, cut:*
2 strips, 10½" x 40½"
24 strips, 2" x 10"
24 strips, 2" x 14"

From the dark print, cut:
7 binding strips, 2½" x 42"

Refer to cutting diagram.

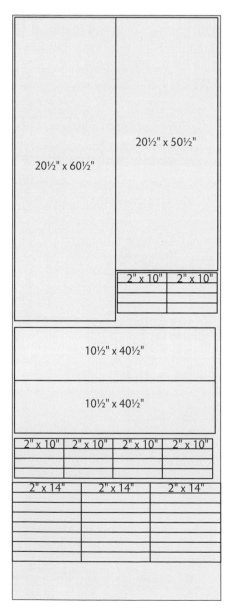

Cutting diagram

BLOCK ASSEMBLY

1. Lay out similar-colored scraps in an appealing design. Not all fabrics will fit into the final design, but you'll find it helpful to have multiple fabrics to choose from.

2. Join the smaller scraps first. Press the seam allowances toward the outside or the section with fewer seams. Trim the excess fabric to even the edges for the next strip or section.

3. In the same manner, continue adding strips or sections, making sure to press and trim after each addition. The block center is complete when the sides measure between 8½" and 10". Make 12 block centers.

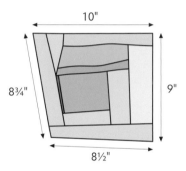

4. Sew gray 2" x 10" strips to the sides of each block center. Press the seam allowances toward the gray strips. Trim the excess fabric to even the edges for the next strips.

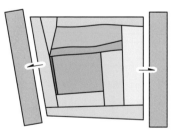

Attach sides and trim.

5. Sew gray 2" x 14" strips to the top and bottom of each block. Press the seam allowances toward the gray strips.

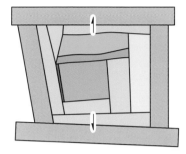

Attach top and bottom.

6. Lay a 10½" square ruler on top of the completed block. Rotate the ruler slightly to skew the placement of the center square; keep in mind you'll need a ¼" seam allowance all around the outside of the block. Trim the block to measure 10½" x 10½".

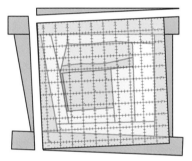

Most of the blocks in the sample quilt are roughly based on simple designs or traditional blocks.

Log Cabin block: Use a traditional log-cabin design as a starting point for any improv block. Build the block in a clockwise direction, adding borders around a wonky center square. Cut strips on an angle.

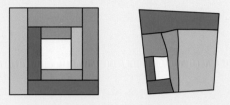

Log Cabin blocks

Courthouse Steps block: Add borders of various fabrics to the sides first, and then to the top and bottom of a pieced center section.

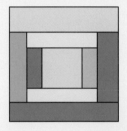
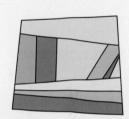

Courthouse Steps blocks

String block: This block is simply made of long strips of fabric cut with curves or wonky angles. It's the simplest style of block shown in this quilt.

String blocks

QUILT ASSEMBLY

1. Arrange the blocks in four rows of three blocks each. When you are pleased with the arrangement, sew the blocks together into rows. Press the seam allowances in opposite directions from row to row.

2. Join the rows. Press the seam allowances in one direction.

3. Sew a gray 10½" x 40½" strip to the right side of the quilt center. Press the seam allowances toward the border. Referring to the assembly diagram, sew the remaining gray strips to the bottom, left side, and top of the quilt top; press.

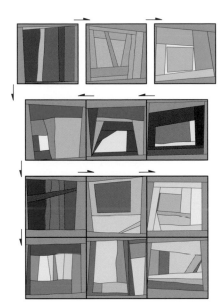

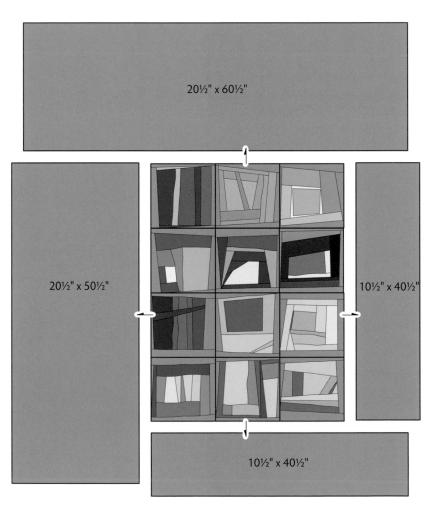

20½" x 60½"

20½" x 50½"

10½" x 40½"

10½" x 40½"

Quilt assembly

FINISHING THE QUILT

For free, downloadable, illustrated how-to instructions on any finishing techniques, go to ShopMartingale.com/HowtoQuilt.

1. Layer the quilt top, batting, and backing; baste the layers together. Quilt as desired.

2. Bind the quilt using the dark-print binding strips. Add a label.

❝ | Optional Pieced Backing

1. From your scraps, cut 32 to 38 rectangles, 2" to 4" wide x 10" long. Sew the rectangles together along their long edges to make a 76"-long strip.

2. From a solid fabric, cut one 40" x 76" piece and two 18" x 42" pieces. Trim the selvage off one end of each 18"-wide piece, then sew the pieces end to end. Press the seam allowances open and trim to 18" x 76".

3. Join the solid pieces and the pieced strip to complete the quilt back.

Designer Bio

KATI SPENCER

FromTheBlueChair.com

Creative outlets have always been extremely important to me. I've moved through various hobbies in my life including sewing, cross-stitch, photography, and other crafty endeavors. I always have a number of projects in process.

When my twins were six months old and my older daughter was just over two, they all settled into the same afternoon napping schedule. With three free hours each afternoon during nap time, I began searching for a new hobby to enjoy and discovered a certain quilting blog with a how-to video on free-motion quilting. I realized I could do that on my sewing machine—I even had the necessary presser foot. I made my first "real" quilt within a few weeks and was instantly hooked. Since then, I've always machine quilted my own quilts. I love seeing the process through from beginning to end.

Soon after, I entered the blogging world and began sharing my projects. I've found an open and accepting community of wonderful quilters online, and learned how to quilt almost exclusively through others' blogs. I'm always inspired when I view the diversity of quilts people make.

I rarely follow patterns and enjoy the freedom to create whatever comes to my mind. I'm constantly sketching and creating quilt ideas in my head. Few of these sketches make it into fabric, but it's fun to experiment and dream up ideas.

LANTERNS IN THE CITY

Designed and pieced by Audrie Bidwell;
quilted by Laura McCarrick

FINISHED QUILT: 66½" x 77½"
FINISHED BLOCKS: 11" x 11"

✳ This quilt is a fun and updated version of the traditional Courthouse Steps pattern. I love how visually stunning the "lanterns" are in this design, and I wanted to make it all the more different by making the quilt look as if there were lanterns around a city block. It reminds me of lantern festivals I went to when I was growing up in Singapore.

MATERIALS

Yardage is based on 42"-wide fabric.

½ yard *each* of 13 assorted solids for Lantern blocks
⅝ yard *each* of 5 assorted solids for Lantern blocks and City block
¼ yard of white solid for block centers and City block border
⅔ yard of gray print for binding
4¾ yards of fabric for backing
72" x 83" piece of batting

GETTING STARTED

Using pieces of paper or masking tape, label all of the assorted solid colors with numbers from 1 to 18. Make a copy of the design sheet on page 83. Decide where you want to place your fabrics and mark the fabric numbers on your design sheet. The sheet will make fabric placement easier whether you have a design wall or not.

The grayed areas on the sheet are section A and the white areas are section B. For each block, you'll need two of each section.

Referring to the City block diagram on page 81 for placement guidance, label the five City block fabrics C to G.

CUTTING

Repeat the cutting directions for the section A and section B fabrics to make 38 blocks, keeping the fabrics for each block in separate piles.

For Each Lantern Block:

From *each* of 2 section A fabrics, cut:
1 strip, 1½" x 42", cut into:
    1 rectangle, 1½" x 3½" (2 total)
    1 rectangle, 1½" x 5½" (2 total)
    1 rectangle, 1½" x 7½" (2 total)
    1 rectangle, 1½" x 9½" (2 total)
    1 rectangle, 1½" x 11½" (2 total)

From *each* of 2 section B fabrics, cut:
1 strip, 1½" x 42"; cut into:
    1 square, 1½" x 1½" (2 total)
    1 rectangle, 1½" x 3½" (2 total)
    1 rectangle, 1½" x 5½" (2 total)
    1 rectangle, 1½" x 7½" (2 total)
    1 rectangle, 1½" x 9½" (2 total)

Continued on page 80

For Block Centers and City Block Border

From the white solid, cut:
2 strips, 1½" x 42"; cut into 39 squares, 1½" x 1½"
2 strips, 1" x 21½"
2 strips, 1" x 22½"

For the City Block

From fabric C, cut:
2 rectangles, 1½" x 2½"
2 rectangles, 2½" x 5½"

From fabric D, cut:
2 rectangles, 2½" x 5½"
2 rectangles, 2½" x 9½"

From fabric E, cut:
2 rectangles, 2½" x 9½"
2 rectangles, 2½" x 13½"

From fabric F, cut:
2 rectangles, 2½" x 13½"
2 rectangles, 2½" x 17½"

From fabric G, cut:
2 rectangles, 2½" x 17½"
2 rectangles, 2½" x 21½"

For the Binding

From the gray print, cut:
8 binding strips, 2½" x 42"

LANTERN BLOCK ASSEMBLY

Each block is constructed from two A sections and two B sections. Each section is made using the square and rectangles from one color; make sure the placement of the first piece in each section is correct before proceeding. After sewing each seam, press the seam allowances toward the newly added piece.

1. Sew section B 1½" squares to opposite sides of a white square. Then add section A 1½" x 3½" rectangles to the center unit as shown.

2. Sew section B 1½" x 3½" rectangles to the unit from step 1.

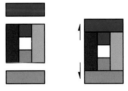

3. Continue adding section A rectangles and then section B rectangles, ending with section A 1½" x 11½" rectangles. Repeat the process to make 38 blocks total.

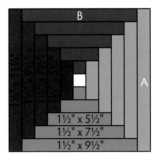

Make 38.

CITY BLOCK ASSEMBLY

After sewing each seam, press the seam allowances toward the newly added rectangle.

1. Sew fabric C 1½" x 2½" rectangles to opposite sides of a white square. Then add fabric C 2½" x 5½" rectangles to the center unit as shown.

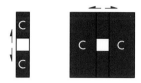

2. Sew fabric D 2½" x 5½" rectangles to opposite sides of the unit from step 1. Then add fabric D 2½" x 9½" rectangles to the unit as shown.

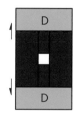

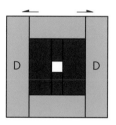

3. Continue adding rectangles in the same manner, ending with fabric G 2½" x 21½" rectangles, making sure each round of rectangles consists of only one fabric. The block should measure 21½" x 21½".

4. Sew white 1" x 21½" strips to opposite sides of the block. Then add white 1" x 22½" strips to the two remaining sides to complete the block. The block should now measure 22½" x 22½".

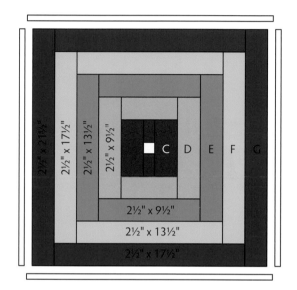

> **❝ | Keep the Blocks Organized**
>
> If you don't have a design wall, you may want to join the blocks in each row as you go. That way it's easier to keep the blocks in the proper order.

QUILT ASSEMBLY

1. Referring to your design sheet and the assembly diagram on page 82, lay out the blocks as shown.

2. Join the blocks in rows 1, 2, 3, 6, and 7. Press the seam allowances in the opposite direction from row to row.

3. For rows 4 and 5, join two blocks vertically and then sew them to the left of the City block. Sew two rows of three blocks each together, and then join the rows. Sew the two-row section to the right of the City block to complete the center section.

4. Join rows 1–3 to make the top section. Join rows 6 and 7 to make the bottom section. Then join the three sections to complete the quilt top. Press the seam allowances in one direction.

FINISHING THE QUILT

For free, downloadable, illustrated how-to instructions on any finishing techniques, go to ShopMartingale.com/HowtoQuilt.

1. Layer the quilt top, batting, and backing; baste the layers together. Quilt as desired.

2. Bind the quilt using the gray binding strips. Add a label.

> **❝ | Designer Bio**
>
> **AUDRIE BIDWELL** BlueIsBleu.blogspot.com
> You'll find Audrie's biography on page 71.

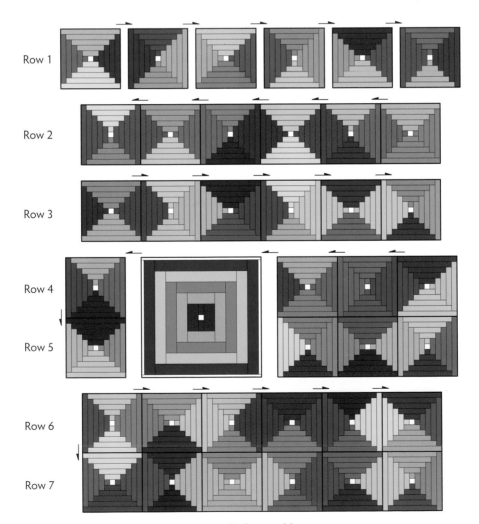

Row 1
Row 2
Row 3
Row 4
Row 5
Row 6
Row 7

Quilt assembly

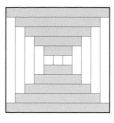

11" block

Design sheet

ACROSS THE QUAD

Designed and made by
Jennifer Mathis

FINISHED QUILT: 63½" x 63½"

✱ "Across the Quad" is a modern take on the classic patchwork quilt. Bright pops of color bounce against the cool gray as your eye wanders along the patchwork path. This quilt would be great for a teenager or adult and could easily take on a more masculine tone by altering the patchwork palette.

MATERIALS

Yardage is based on 42"-wide fabric.

2⅜ yards of gray solid for background

75 assorted 5" squares of bright prints for patchwork

⅝ yard of multicolor-striped fabric for binding

4 yards of fabric for backing*

69" x 69" piece of batting

*Or see "Optional Pieced Backing" on page 87.

CUTTING

From the *lengthwise grain* of the gray solid, cut:*

1 strip, 23" x 36½" (G)

2 strips, 9½" x 36½" (J, K)

1 strip, 9½" x 23" (I)

1 strip, 5" x 9½" (H)

1 strip, 9½" x 14" (L)

1 strip, 14" x 41" (M)

From the multicolor-striped fabric, cut:

7 binding strips, 2½" x 42"

*Refer to cutting diagram.

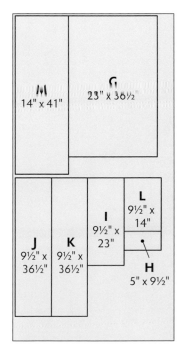

Cutting diagram

QUILT ASSEMBLY

The quilt is constructed in sections. Before assembly, lay out the assorted squares on a design wall or on the floor as shown in the assembly diagram. Arrange the squares so that you don't have like fabrics side by side.

1. For section A, sew three squares together to make a row. Make eight rows, pressing the seam allowances in opposite directions from row to row. Join the rows, carefully matching the seam intersections. Press the seam allowances in one direction.

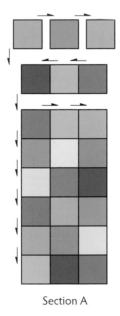

Section A

2. Repeat step 1, sewing the squares together to make the following sections:

- Section B: Two rows of two squares each
- Section C: Three rows of three squares each
- Section D: Three rows of two squares each
- Section F: Three rows of three squares each

3. For section E, sew three rows of three squares each. Join the three rows to make a nine-patch unit. Make three of these units. Then sew the units together to complete section E.

4. Referring to the assembly diagram, lay out sections A–F and gray strips G–M as shown. Sew the H and I strips to opposite sides of section B. Then add the J strip to the right edge and the G strip to the left edge of the three-piece section. Press the seam allowances toward the gray after adding each strip.

5. Sew the K strip to the left edge of section A. Then join this two-piece section to the partial row from step 4 to complete the top section of the quilt top.

6. Sew sections D, C, and E together to make the center section. Press the seam allowances toward section C.

7. Sew the L strip to the left edge of section F. Then sew the M strip to the right edge of section F to complete the bottom section. Press the seam allowances toward the gray strips.

8. Join the three sections to complete the quilt top. Press the seam allowances away from the center patchwork section. Trim and square up the corners as needed.

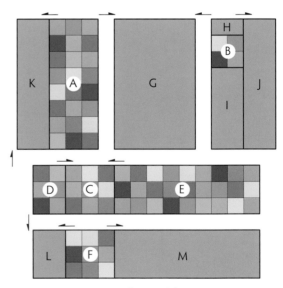

Quilt assembly

FINISHING THE QUILT

For free, downloadable, illustrated how-to instructions on any finishing techniques, go to ShopMartingale.com/HowtoQuilt.

1. Layer the quilt top, batting, and backing; baste the layers together. Quilt as desired.

2. Bind the quilt using the multicolor-striped binding strips. Add a label.

❝ | Optional Pieced Backing

For the pieced backing, you'll need 22 assorted 5" squares, 3⅛ yards of gray solid, and 1½ yards of white solid.

1. Join 16 squares to make a patchwork square measuring 18½" x 18½". Join the remaining squares to make a patchwork rectangle measuring 9½" x 14".

2. From the gray solid, cut one 26" x 69" piece and two 17" x 42" pieces. Trim the selvage off one end of each 17"-wide piece; then sew the pieces end to end. Press the seam allowances open and trim to 17" x 69".

3. From the white solid, cut one 18½" x 33½" piece, one 18½" x 18½" square, one 9½" x 21" piece, and one 9½" x 35½" piece. Sew the 18½"-wide pieces to opposite sides of the patchwork square. Sew the 9½"-wide pieces to opposite sides of the patchwork rectangle. Join these two strips to make the center section of the backing.

4. Join the gray pieces and the center section to complete the quilt back.

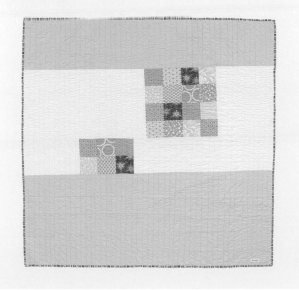

Designer Bio
JENNIFER MATHIS
EllisonLane.blogspot.com

I'm a Southern girl, a former teacher, and now a home engineer (aka Mama). I'm a mother to two precious young children, a girl and a boy, and wife to a super supportive husband who understands and encourages my creative pursuits. I'm a self-taught sewist and quilter, slightly obsessed with sewing, design, and modern fabric. I'm driven by a need to express myself visually, a love of fabric and design, and the thrill that comes from creating something beautiful from a sketch and an idea.

I taught myself to sew and quilt from online tutorials and the more I was drawn to the online quilting community, the more I wanted to be a part of it. I now share my ideas, designs, projects, and interests on my blog, Ellison Lane Quilts, and have sewing friends from Japan to Ireland to Morocco and everywhere in between, all because we share a passion for quilting and sewing.

Modern quilting inspires and excites me because it's the perfect outlet for creative expression and blends the past with the future in a tangible form of comfort. I'm so inspired by modern quilting and sewing that I formed the Charlotte, North Carolina, chapter of the Modern Quilt Guild. I love being able to share my enthusiasm with others in person and help the modern quilting community grow.

CANDY NECKLACE

Designed and made by
Lee Heinrich

FINISHED QUILT: 58½" x 66½"
FINISHED BLOCKS: 6" x 6"

✳ If you've already got the hang of half-square triangles, quarter-square triangles will be a piece of cake—and they'll expand your design possibilities! The quarter-square triangles in this quilt give the look of beveled edges and allow for fun color combinations.

MATERIALS

Yardage is based on 42"-wide fabric.

⅜ yard *each* of 7 assorted coral prints for blocks
2⅛ yards of gray solid for background
¼ yard *each* of 7 assorted green prints for blocks
¼ yard *each* of 7 assorted blue prints for blocks
⅝ yard of green print for binding
3¾ yards of fabric for backing
64" x 72" piece of batting
4" or 6" bias-square ruler

CUTTING

You may want to cut the 2½" squares and 2½"-wide rectangles first; then lay out the quilt, minus the quarter-square-triangle units. That way, you can arrange the 3½" squares and determine how many squares to cut from each print to achieve the design you want.

From the green prints for blocks, cut *a total of*:
18 squares, 3½" x 3½"
39 rectangles, 2½" x 6½"

From the blue prints, cut *a total of*:
18 squares, 3½" x 3½"
39 rectangles, 2½" x 6½"

From the *lengthwise grain* of the gray solid, cut:
13 strips, 2½" x 72"; cut into:
    8 strips, 2½" x 66½"
    39 rectangles, 2½" x 6½"
    38 squares, 2½" x 2½"
2 strips, 3½" x 72"; cut into 36 squares, 3½" x 3½"
6 squares, 3" x 3"; cut in half diagonally to yield 12 triangles

From the coral prints, cut *a total of*:
76 squares, 3½" x 3½"
152 squares, 2½" x 2½"

From the green print, cut:
7 binding strips, 2½" x 42"

BLOCK A ASSEMBLY

1. Layer each green or blue square with a gray 3½" square, right sides together. Mark a diagonal line on the wrong side of the lighter square. Stitch ¼" on each side of the marked line.

2. Cut the squares apart on the line. Then, without moving the squares, cut diagonally in the other direction to make four quarter-square triangles. Flip the triangles open and press the seam allowances to one side.

3. Repeat steps 1 and 2, using two coral 3½" squares to make four quarter-square triangles.

4. With right sides together, layer one triangle unit from step 2 with a triangle unit from step 3 and align the opposing seams. (Re-press the seam allowances, if needed, to create opposing seam allowances.) Sew along the long edges and press the seam allowances open. (See "Pinless Quarter-Square Triangles" for piecing tips.) Repeat the process to make 70 quarter-square-triangle units from each fabric combination. You'll have two gray/blue triangle units and two gray/green triangle units left over; discard or set these aside for another project. You'll use the 12 coral triangle units left over to make block C.

Make 70 of each.

> **" | Pinless Quarter-Square Triangles**
>
> Using pins to sew your quarter-square triangles is time-consuming and can distort your seams. To accurately piece the final seam of your quarter-square-triangle units without pins, layer two triangle units, right sides together. Make sure the existing seams are pressed in opposite directions so that you can "lock" the seams together snugly, aligning the raw edges of the half units. Press the two units together, one on top of the other, to "marry" the two units and prevent them from slipping around as you sew.

5. Using a bias-square ruler, place the 45° line on one of the seam lines and align the 1¼" lines on the ruler with the center point on a quarter-square-triangle unit. Trim the units to measure 2½" x 2½".

6. Arrange four quarter-square-triangle units, four coral 2½" squares, and one gray 2½" square as shown. Sew the pieces together in rows. Press the seam allowances toward the coral squares. Join the rows to complete the block. Press the seam allowances toward the center. Repeat to make a total of 32 blocks. You'll use the remaining quarter-square-triangle units to make block C.

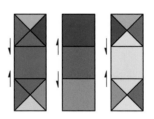

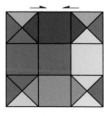

Block A
Make 32.

BLOCK B ASSEMBLY

Join one green rectangle, one gray rectangle, and one blue rectangle along their long edges as shown. Press the seam allowances toward the outside rectangles. Make 39 blocks.

Block B
Make 39.

BLOCK C ASSEMBLY

1. Sew a coral quarter-square-triangle unit to a gray 3" triangle as shown. Press the seam allowances toward the gray triangle. Make 12 of these units.

Make 12.

2. Arrange two quarter-square-triangle units, two units from step 1, four coral 2½" squares, and one gray 2½" square as shown. Sew the pieces together in rows. Press the seam allowances toward the coral squares. Join the rows to complete the block. Press the seam allowances toward the center. Repeat to make six blocks total.

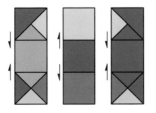

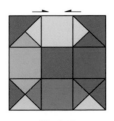

Block C
Make 6.

Just me and my modern quilts.

Designer Bio
LEE HEINRICH
FreshlyPieced.blogspot.com

I've been quilting and sewing for four years, and blogging about it for a little over a year. I live in Milwaukee, Wisconsin, with my husband and two daughters. I began my career as a news reporter and editor, and later made the switch to graphic design. After designing everything from newsletters to logos to wedding invitations, I quit work to stay home with my oldest daughter. It was around that time that I got a hand-me-down, avocado-green Kenmore sewing machine from my mom, and it wasn't long before I was reading everything I could find about sewing and quilting. In fact, I owe almost all I know about quilting to other bloggers.

I see modern quilting as an extension of my design work—design rendered in fabric instead of on paper or on a computer screen. A design that you can literally wrap up in to keep yourself warm—it doesn't get much better than that!

Blogging about my sewing exploits appeals to the former reporter in me. The ability to write quickly and on a daily basis has served me well. But more than anything, I love the connection my blog has given me to like-minded quilters all over the world. I see the blog as my side of an ongoing conversation with readers about the world of modern quilting.

QUILT ASSEMBLY

1. Arrange the blocks in seven vertical rows of 11 blocks each, alternating and rotating the blocks as shown in the assembly diagram. Notice that rows 1, 3, 5, and 7 begin and end with B blocks; rows 2, 4, and 6 begin and end with C blocks.

2. Sew the blocks together in rows. Press the seam allowances toward the B blocks.

3. Join the rows, alternating them with the gray 66½"-long sashing strips. Sew a gray strip to each side as a border. Press the seam allowances toward the gray strips.

FINISHING THE QUILT

For free, downloadable, illustrated how-to instructions on any finishing techniques, go to ShopMartingale.com/HowtoQuilt.

1. Layer the quilt top, batting, and backing; baste the layers together. Quilt as desired.

2. Bind the quilt using the green binding strips. Add a label.

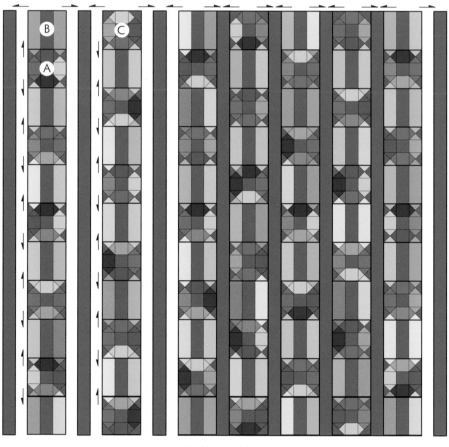

Quilt assembly

SCATTERED

Designed and quilted by Allison Harris;
pieced by Amber Hoffman

FINISHED QUILT: 60½" x 72½"
FINISHED BLOCKS: 6" x 6"

✳ One simple block is all you need to make this eye-catching quilt. The bright triangles add just enough color to "pop" against the solid background. Try adding a bold backing to complement the simple front and add a touch of surprise.

MATERIALS

Yardage is based on 42"-wide fabric.

4 yards of gray solid for block backgrounds
60 assorted 5" squares of bright prints for blocks
⅝ yard of green-striped fabric for binding
3¾ yards of fabric for backing
66" x 78" piece of batting

CUTTING

From the gray solid, cut:
8 strips, 5" x 42"; cut into 60 squares, 5" x 5"
35 strips, 2½" x 42"; cut into:
    120 rectangles, 2½" x 4½"
    120 rectangles, 2½" x 6½"

From the green-striped fabric, cut:
7 binding strips, 2½" x 42"

BLOCK ASSEMBLY

1. Mark a diagonal line on the wrong side of each gray square. Layer the marked square with a bright square, right sides together, and stitch ¼" on each side of the marked line. Cut the squares apart on the line to make two half-square-triangle units. Press the seam allowances toward the darker triangle. Trim the units to measure 4½" x 4½". Make 120 units total.

Make 120.

2. Sew a gray 2½" x 4½" rectangle to each half-square-triangle unit as shown. Press the seam allowances toward the rectangle. Make 120.

Make 120.

3. Sew a gray 2½" x 6½" rectangle to each unit from step 2 as shown to complete the blocks. Press the seam allowances toward the rectangle. Make 120 blocks. The blocks should measure 6½" x 6½".

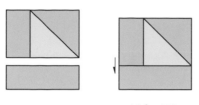

Make 120.

QUILT ASSEMBLY

1. Lay out the blocks in 12 rows of 10 blocks each, rotating every other block in each row as shown in the assembly diagram. Sew the blocks together in rows. Press the seam allowances in opposite directions from row to row.

2. Join the rows. Press the seam allowances in one direction.

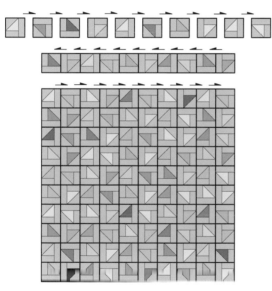

Quilt assembly

FINISHING THE QUILT

For free, downloadable, illustrated how-to instructions on any finishing techniques, go to ShopMartingale.com/HowtoQuilt.

1. Layer the quilt top, batting, and backing; baste the layers together. Quilt as desired.

2. Bind the quilt using the green-striped binding strips. Add a label.

Designer Bio
ALLISON HARRIS
CluckCluckSew.com

For the past few years, I've shared tidbits of my quilts, fumbles, and family life through blogging. My blog was started as a way to keep a record of the things I was making and selling, but it has become a way of sharing what I make with others and a networking tool to meet other quilters with my same aesthetic. Even though I'm a busy mom of three, I'm thankful for the bits of time I have to sew, blog, and connect with fellow quilters around the world.

My style of quilting has been referred to as modern, but I've never agreed with the idea of "modern quilting." Most of my inspiration comes from antique quilts made with traditional patterns.

I find it exciting and inspirational that quilting is becoming popular again with younger generations like mine. There is no doubt that blogging and social networking have played a huge part in the revival of quilting, and hopefully it will continue for many years to come. I love that I can share what I make with my blog readers and people who love the same things I do. It's truly a support group and a connection I'm lucky enough to have with thousands of people I've never even met.